NAZI WAR CRIMINALS

NAZI WAR CRIMINALS

BY ELAINE LANDAU

FRANKLIN WATTS
New York/London/Toronto/Sydney/1990

All photographs courtesy of Wide World Photos.

Library of Congress Cataloging-in-Publication Data
Landau, Elaine.
Nazi war criminals / by Elaine Landau.
p.   cm.
Summary: Examines the cases of several Nazi war criminals,
describing the charges against them, and how they have been brought
to justice.
Includes bibliographical references.
ISBN 0-531-15181-6—ISBN 0-531-10957-7 (lib. bdg.)
1. War criminals—Europe—Juvenile literature.   2. World War,
1939–1945—Atrocities—Juvenile literature.   3. Criminal
investigation—Juvenile literature.   [1. War criminals.   2. World
War, 1939–1945—Atrocities.]   I. Title.
D803.L36   1990
364.1'38'0922—dc20   90-12533   CIP   AC

For Karl and Regina Diamant,
who survived the Nazi camps to find
renewed life and joy in America

CONTENTS

NAZI WAR CRIMINALS

Introduction

During Hitler's reign in World War II, six million
Jews, nearly two-thirds of all the Jews in Europe,
were murdered because of the racial obsessions of
a madman. His plan had been to completely annihilate the Jewish people. Other people were sense-
lessly and brutally killed as well. As stated in the
article, "The Gentile Holocaust," which appeared
in the magazine *America*, "Also 9 to 10 million Slavs
(Poles, Ukrainians, Russians) were annihilated—not
in the war, but purposely—for precisely the same
reasons. The number is staggering, but it does not
include the half million Gypsies who were also executed, incinerated, or worked to death from 1933
to 1945. Nor does it include the hundreds of thousands who were murdered quickly or slowly, because they were Jehovah's Witnesses or homosexuals."[1]

At first, the Nazis engaged in subtle humiliations
and tortures—"A favorite amusement of Nazi mobs
was forcing Jewish men and women to go down on
their hands and knees and scrub the pavements with

This Jewish man resists the Nazis as they force him to push a heavy cart of cleaning materials through the streets.

As of September 1941, Jews in Berlin, Germany, were required by law to wear a six pointed yellow star inscribed with the word Jude (Jew) on their clothing. Here a Jewish couple walk to their home in Berlin.

acid preparations which bit into the skin, so that they had to go straight to the hospital for treatment."[2]

Later, when the murder of innocent people became an accepted part of the Nazi workday, toddlers were sometimes tossed alive into bonfires. After the war and killing were finally over, some of those guilty of atrocities were tried and punished. Others who were captured chose to take their own lives rather than face the consequences of their deeds. Yet, still other Nazi war criminals escaped from Europe to different parts of the world. Even today, many of these individuals who have evaded justice continue to lead comfortable lives.

There are groups of individuals throughout the world, however, who are determined to disrupt the pleasurable lives of World War II criminals who now disguise themselves as model citizens and neighbors. Beate Klarsfeld is a German-born woman who has devoted much of her life to tracking down Nazi war criminals. She's stated that she does so precisely "because I am not Jewish, but German. My generation—symbolically the children of the Nazis—has a special duty to fight anti-Semitism and to help Jews who are being persecuted today. . . . The young generation—the children of the Holocaust survivors—are now strong enough to demand the justice that their parents were too weak to seek. Criminals who weren't big Nazi names generally escaped punishment right after the war."[3]

Simon Wiesenthal, who has been hunting Nazi war criminals since the end of World War II, continues his work out of a three-room office in Vienna, Austria. Wiesenthal, whose work is supported by contributions from around the world, is aided in his efforts by four or five young assistants. Simon Wie-

This is the courtroom in Nuremberg, Germany, where some Nazi war criminals were tried for their crimes against humanity. The trials lasted from 1945 to 1949.

Renowned Nazi hunter Beate Klarsfeld (left) announces her plans to continue her work. She is photographed with Menachem Rosensaft, founding chairman of the International Network of Children of Jewish Holocaust Survivors and New York–elected representative Elizabeth Holtzman.

senthal and his wife are the sole survivors of ninety-one family members who perished in Nazi death camps.

Wiesenthal says that the forever silenced voices of the Holocaust victims keep him at his work of bringing their murderers to justice. As he's stated, "My wife has often asked me if I have not done enough. But I am still convinced that I survived to represent and to speak for those who did not—and that job is never done."[4]

JOSEF MENGELE —
THE ANGEL OF DEATH

SS officer Dr. Josef Mengele arrived at the Auschwitz concentration camp in May 1943. The tremendous camp stretched for miles, imprisoning nearly a hundred and fifty thousand individuals. The area was bounded with barbed wire and stalked by SS guard dogs.

Auschwitz contained five crematoria and gas chambers. As many as nine thousand Jews might be gassed within twenty-four hours. The flames and thick black smoke that spread from the crematoria chimneys could be seen for nearly thirty miles. The air surrounding the camp reeked with the nauseating stench of charred human flesh and hair.

Auschwitz served a dual purpose for Hitler's regime. It functioned as a center for mass extermination as well as a slave-labor camp to supply a continuous pool of workers for German companies involved in the war effort.

The strongest of the incoming prisoners were allowed to live only to be worked to death. Inmates who collapsed while at work were often cruelly

Fresh flowers are placed here in memory of those who died in this German crematorium. These transport carts were used to remove bodies.

beaten or kicked to determine if there was any life left in them. Most of the inmate laborers were Jews, although there were also Russians, Poles, some Allied prisoners of war, and Germans who had vocally objected to the policies of the Third Reich.

Living conditions at Auschwitz were intolerable. In the work details, more than four hundred prisoners were crowded into an area intended for one hundred and sixty individuals. Three people had to share a wooden bunk meant for one. The bed's only covering was a filthy layer of straw. The workers' block was also rampant with dysentery. As the situation was described in the book *Less Than Slaves*:

> Inmates were literally being worked to death. They were forced to run while unloading heavy cement bags weighing more than one hundred pounds. Drinking water was contaminated, clothing was sparse, and the food was totally inadequate. Many died of freezing or starvation. The conditions for all forced laborers were terrible. But by far, the worst were the conditions for the Jews.[1]

In contrast, SS officers such as Josef Mengele lived at Auschwitz in relative comfort. They enjoyed the luxury of such extra rations as a dozen cigarettes a day, a one-fifth liter of vodka, and snacks of German sausage. The officers also enjoyed delicious meals served up by the chefs at the Waffen SS club.

Josef Mengele was only at the camp a short time before gaining a reputation for being excessively devoted to the especially inhumane aspects of his work. While some of the German doctors did only what was required of them, Mengele seemed tireless in his pursuits.

Mengele was particularly zealous in sending newly arrived inmates to the gas chambers. In fact,

These dying concentration camp victims
were given nearly nothing to eat. Many died
of starvation before they could be gassed.

he'd been described at the camp as the chief provider for the gas chambers and cremating ovens. Each time a new transport arrived, two camp doctors were assigned the duty of examining the human cargo. Deciding who would live and who would be killed was a gruesome task. Although many of the doctors had to get drunk before they appeared on the ramp to make the selections, Mengele did so with a cold, cynical eye.

Immaculately groomed in his fitted SS uniform with glistening black boots and polished cane, Mengele was often the first person many prisoners saw when arriving at Auschwitz. With a detached and haughty air, he executed the power of life and death as he made his selections. Often, he whistled a tune from an opera as he cruelly went about his work: "Day after day he'd appear at his post, watching the pitiful crowds of men, women and children struggle past, exhausted from their excruciating journey to Auschwitz while crowded in a cattle car. He (Mengele) would point his cane at each person and direct them with one word: 'right' or 'left'. . . . He seemed to enjoy his grisly task."[2]

More so than any of the other SS, Mengele was remembered by surviving inmates as being present when selections took place. In 1964, when twenty-two Auschwitz defendants were on trial for war crimes, inmate survivor Ari Fuks, who had been assigned to work at the arrival ramps, reported that he continually saw Mengele at the railway. When questioned by the judge as to how much time Mengele could have possibly spent selecting those who would die, the camp survivor answered, "In my opinion, always. Night and day."[3]

The West German indictment later issued for

Josef Mengele lists witnesses who testified that Mengele was present at a minimum of thirty-nine separate selections within a four-month period, sending tens of thousands of Jews to their death in the gas chambers.[4] In actuality, the real figure may be significantly higher, since in many instances there were no surviving witnesses.

Mengele was also extremely active in ridding the camp of workers who'd become ill or less useful to the regime. The West German indictment documented his activities in this area:

> Josef Mengele is accused of having actively and decisively taken part in selections in the prisoners' sick blocks, of such prisoners who through hunger, deprivation, exhaustion, sickness, disease, abuse or other reasons were unfit for work in the camp. . . . Those selected were killed either through injections or firing squads or by painful suffocation to death through prussic acid in the gas chambers in order to make room in the camp for the "fit" prisoners, selected by him or other SS doctors in the aforementioned fashion. The injections that killed were made with phenol, petrol, Evipal, chloroform or air into the circulation, especially into the heart chamber, either with his own hands or he ordered the SS sanitary worker to do it while he watched. He is alleged to have also supervised, in cases of camp and hospital block selections, when SS sanitary workers threw granules of prussic acid formula Zyklon-B into the inlet pipes of the rooms with people condemned to die hemmed together, or he threw it himself.[5]

Mengele, who considered himself a scientist as well as a doctor, was especially interested in finding pairs of twins who arrived at the camp. At times, he'd greet the arriving transports shouting, *"Zwillinge, Zwillinge, Zwillinge!"* ("Twins, twins, twins!")

Mengele wanted the twins in order to conduct a series of experiments on them. The SS doctor was an ardent racist. It was his hope to find the key to preserving the best qualities of what he believed was a blond, blue-eyed, Aryan superrace.

To Mengele, Auschwitz was a human laboratory overflowing with free specimens on which to conduct his often ghoulish research experiments. As stated in the West German indictment against Mengele: "The accused Josef Mengele is charged with having carried out medical experiments on living prisoners for scientific publication out of ambition and personal career progression. He fully intended the victim to die according to the manner of the experiment and valued their lives cheaply. They often died merely to further his medical knowledge and academic education."[6]

Mengele had a special pathology laboratory built into Crematorium 2, where the freshly gassed victims could be conveniently dissected. Some of Mengele's grisly experiments were especially difficult to comprehend. Among these were Mengele's attempts to change eye color by injecting different-color dyes into the eyes of children. The rationale behind the procedure was to develop a blue-eyed race of people. The dye injections resulted in painful infections and, in some cases, blindness. Once the tests were completed and the children were no longer of any use to Mengele, he had them gassed.

Often children were experimented on by Mengele while they were still conscious. Without the use of anesthetics, the German doctor performed crude surgery as well as other experiments. Limbs were amputated without cause, and at times children were injected with typhus. At Auschwitz, Dr. Josef Mengele soon became known for his unquenchable thirst for performing experiments on human beings. The inmates referred to him as "the Angel of Death." His sinister silhouette might appear at the barracks at any hour of the day or night when he fell short of readily available victims.

The blatant cruelty and horror of which Mengele was capable seemed limitless. At one point, he had over three hundred small children thrown into an open fire to be burned alive. The children screamed, and some managed to crawl out from the burning pit, but an officer circled the fire with a large stick and pushed them back in.[7]

As World War II continued, millions of inmates in concentration camps such as Auschwitz met hideous deaths. There was no hope of mercy from their captors and, for the most part, little chance of immediate rescue by Allied forces. Despite the fact that Allied warplanes bombed some industrial installations very near Auschwitz, they never bombed the camp or the railway tracks by which persons were transported to the camp. The bright flames of the burning ovens would have provided excellent targets. Since inmates were housed far from the crematoria, the loss of life might have been negligible.

But it never happened. Instead, as it became clear that Germany was going to lose the war, Mengele moved quickly to cover up evidence of his experiments. In addition, the SS had orders to destroy charts and records and to blow up the ovens to further erase any tangible proof of what had occurred at the camp.

Mengele knew it was essential that he leave the camp before the Allies arrived. Under cover of darkness, on the night of January 17, 1945, Josef Mengele departed from Auschwitz forever. As the artillery of the Allied forces raged in the distance, Mengele began his new life as a fugitive from justice.

Mengele decided to head westward. He shed his SS uniform to join a unit of ordinary German soldiers. Hoping to conceal his past actions, he pretended to be just one of the men in the ranks. However, at least one soldier in his new unit thought that Mengele might have a hidden past. In describing the new man's behavior, the soldier noted that each morning at roll call, Mengele gave another name: "He evidently couldn't remember what name he had given the day before, so he must have used four or five additional names. He was secretive and I knew he had to be SS."[8]

Things were to worsen for Mengele; within weeks, his unit was taken by American forces. While the Americans held him in custody, Mengele's true name was revealed to them. Unfortunately, they didn't understand its significance. Since they had no idea that Mengele has been an SS member, he wasn't subjected to a rigorous interrogation of his activities. His name was never checked against a list of wanted war criminals either.

Mengele's personal vanity is partly responsible for his eventual freedom from the Americans. The SS required all its officers to have their blood type tattooed either on their arm or chest. Mengele had insisted on not having his skin marked in any manner. He had previously spent a good deal of time preening himself in front of the mirror, while admiring the smoothness of his own skin. Without the tattoo, the Americans had no reason to suspect that Mengele was anything more than a common soldier.

Meanwhile, as of April 1945, just two months

prior to his capture by the Americans, Mengele had been identified as a principal war criminal as concentration camp survivors began filing statements with the Poles, French, Yugoslavs, British, and Czechs. Dr. Josef Mengele was listed with the United Nations War Crimes Commission as wanted "for mass murder and other crimes." Mengele was also listed on the first Central Registry of War Crimes and Security Suspects (CROWCASS), compiled by the Allied High Command in Paris. The U.S. Judge Advocate General's Office had also amassed substantial evidence against Mengele.

Nevertheless, Mengele was released by the Allies shortly after his capture. To this day, it is not known whether the wanted lists of war criminals ever reached the camp authorities holding Mengele. It's possible that in the chaos immediately following the war, some lists never reached all the detention camps. Besides, due to the tremendous number of individuals involved in the war's aftermath, Americans had a policy of processing prisoners as rapidly as possible. In this way, more Germans were speedily released to begin rebuilding their country.

Once freed by the Americans, Mengele sought work on a farm in the distant German countryside. The farm family who employed him thought that Mengele might be more than a common laborer: "He evidently had to hide. He must have been a Nazi, and we thought he must have been high brass. . . . When he came he had very fine hands. He had never worked before, certainly not on a farm. He didn't know how to milk a cow."[9]

As Mengele hid out on the farm, the predicament of convicted Nazi war criminals worsened. By December 1946, in Nuremberg, Germany, twenty-three

SS physicians and scientists were brought to trial by the Americans. As a result of what is known as the famous "Doctors' Trial," seven of the men were sentenced to death and five others to life imprisonment.

Mengele followed the proceedings with great interest, as did other members of his family. They felt certain that Josef Mengele would end his life on the gallows if he were found and brought to trial. But Mengele managed to elude the authorities. Posing as a farmhand, he resided quietly in Germany for the next four years.

As time passed, to ensure his safety, Mengele fled Germany. Coming from an affluent family of farm machinery manufacturers, Mengele had ample financial resources available to him. Therefore, he was able to bribe officials to secure both an illegal passport and a cabin on a boat to South America.

Mengele's first South American sanctuary was Argentina, which he chose for several reasons. Even prior to the war, a significantly powerful German community had been established there. Following Hitler's rise to power, the area had adopted a strong pro-Nazi slant.

Therefore, following the war, Argentina was receptive to Nazis attempting to evade justice. In addition, when Josef Mengele arrived in Argentina in September 1949, the South American haven was ruled by a dictator who had received substantial payoffs from the Nazi party to ensure the protection of its members.

Even within Argentina's protective environment, however, Mengele still feared that his true identity would be discovered. Since he was particularly fearful that he'd be recognized because of his prominent forehead, he decided to undergo plastic surgery to change his appearance. Mengele insisted on having only a local anesthetic during the surgery so that he could observe the surgeon's work. Dissatisfied with the surgeon's technique, Mengele ordered that the surgery be stopped halfway through the operation. He decided instead that he would always wear a hat whenever he left the house.

Over the next ten years, Mengele led a fairly comfortable life. But then things began to change. By 1958, a newly determined effort to bring Mengele to justice was under way.

During the war, an anti-Nazi political activist named Hermann Langbein had been shipped to Auschwitz. While at the camp, Langbein had been ordered to work as a clerk in the chief physician's office. Having survived the camp, he began to compile a substantial packet of evidence against Mengele.

Unfortunately, once the Allies had passed the responsibility to prosecute war criminals to German authorities, the efforts began to pale. The prosecution record of the newly born Federal Republic of Germany (West Germany) had proved to be exceptionally poor. Now Langbein hoped to publicly embarrass the government in order to set the wheels of justice in productive motion.

Finally, on June 5, 1959, the West German government issued an indictment listing seventeen counts of Mengele's barbarous brutality. The warrant was sent to the West German foreign office in Bonn, so that extradition proceedings from Argentina could be initiated. But it was too late. The search for Mengele in Argentina proved futile, as he had already settled in Paraguay and had applied for citizenship under his own name.

Mengele's stay in Paraguay was filled with a sense of trepidation and uneasiness. The Israelis as well as other independent Nazi hunters had been active in the area, seeking out war criminals. To try to ensure his safety and remain ahead of his would-be captors, Mengele left Paraguay for Brazil.

Relying again on his family's contacts and money, Mengele found a safe refuge on a Brazilian farm with the Stammer family. Using the name Peter Hochbichler, Mengele worked as the Stammers' overseer. He was not well liked by others on the staff. The men under Mengele felt that their boss was often haughty and abusive. Those on the farm found it unusual to have a foreman who read philosophy and history and loved classical music. As one farmhand, Francisci de Souza, described Mengele: "I didn't like him, but I couldn't do anything about it. He loved giving orders and kept saying that we should work more and harder. The worst of it was that he didn't seem to understand much about farming or heavy work."[10]

Mengele was sickened by his life's turn of events. He disliked the farm and found it difficult to adjust to his new lowly status. And although he had again changed his place of residence, he still dreaded the possibility of being captured by the Israelis. Always afraid that his prominent forehead would reveal his identity, Mengele continued to wear a hat, even on the hottest days of the tropical summers. As one of Mengele's co-workers noted, "Whenever I got near him, he pulled his hat down over his face and dug his hands into his pockets."[11] To complicate matters, Mengele did not even get along well with the Stammer family.

Mengele's anxiety was intensified by the news that international efforts for his capture had increased. West Germany had extended its extradition request from Argentina to Brazil. A myth encouraged by sensationalized newspaper and television reports soon began to surround him. Mengele was quickly gaining a reputation as the world's most elusive criminal.

According to the legend, Mengele had nearly supernatural powers of escape. The former Nazi doctor was said to be extremely wealthy, well armed, and protected by a band of assassins. Supposedly, Mengele and his men had foiled a number of Israeli attempts to capture him and had killed several agents in the process. The stories may have sold newspapers, but they were fictitious.

Instead, Mengele continued to hide out on the Stammer farm in an uneasy relationship with his hosts. He was given to erratic mood shifts that were troublesome to everyone around him. One day he'd be sullen, quiet, and brooding, while the next day he'd appear talkative and display a sharp sense of humor.

After a time, Mengele's true identity was revealed to the Stammers, but they didn't turn him in to the authorities. This was probably due to the fact that the Stammers had become financially dependent on their illicit guest. Through his family's wealth, Mengele was able to provide the Stammers with additional funds for their personal use. Besides, as the Stammers' philosophical views were similar to those of the Third Reich, Mengele's attitude and actions were not morally repugnant to them.

Despite his obscure existence on the farm, Mengele never felt safe from Israeli Nazi hunters. His fears were fueled by reports that Israeli agents had secretly sought and abducted other Nazis hiding in South America to be tried and hanged in Israel. Mengele was determined to avoid this fate at all cost.

To safeguard his own security, Mengele never ventured out for a walk without taking a number of dogs with him. Often as many as fifteen dogs flanked his side. Yet even with his protective pack, Mengele never went very far from the farm.

For added protection, Mengele had an eighteen-foot watchtower built. While supervising its construction, Mengele told the farmhands building the tower that it was to serve as a bird-watching station for the Stammer family. But no one except Mengele ever used the tower. He'd remain in it for hours on end, as he scanned the surrounding countryside. The tower afforded Mengele, using binoculars, a clear view of the roads and paths from the nearest town, which was about five miles away. Contrary to the glorified tales of Mengele as a well-armed fugitive surrounded by muscled bodyguards and electrified fences, the man known at Auschwitz as the Angel of Death had only his watchtower for protection. This was a reality that left him haunted by what his eventual fate might be. As he wrote in his diary: "Out of the beautiful house of ideal plans, one stone after the other breaks down, and the final collapse comes nearer and nearer. Occasionally, I dream of a double-headed guillotine."[12]

By the summer of 1962, Mengele was actually considerably safer than he'd imagined. He had fooled the West German government into thinking that he was still in Paraguay rather than in Brazil.

The house in Brazil that Mengele shared with the Stammer family. Notice the tall watchtower that permitted Mengele to spot anyone approaching the property.

As a result, the West German extradition office exerted a good deal of pressure on the Paraguayan government to hand the fugitive over. They hesitated to believe Paraguay's claims that Mengele had left the country, thinking it was merely a ruse to protect him.

At about the same time, Israel's hunt for Mengele lessened, as the young country shifted its priorities. Israel's safety and existence had been threatened by surrounding Arab states, and at that point all its energy needed to be directed toward its own survival. Faced with the threat of annihilation by hostile bordering states, Israel could not afford the time and resources to actively continue its pursuit of Nazi war criminals in distant parts of the world. However, putting aside the hunt was painful, since at that time Israeli intelligence had brought them closer to their desired target than ever before. As one Israeli agent explained: "We would have eventually found Mengele. It was just a question of time. If we had one more year, we'd have got him. Just one more year, and we'd have him in Israel, and he would have hanged."[13]

Although Mengele longed to bury the memory of his Auschwitz deeds because he feared punishment, he was unable to escape his past. In West Germany, a long-running trial of SS Auschwitz personnel, including guards, officers, and doctors, continued. As the gruesome details were focused on, the name of the absent Dr. Mengele kept cropping up. One witness described how selections for the gas chambers were made: "I also remember Dr. König, and to his credit I must say that he always got drunk beforehand, as did Dr. Rhode. Mengele didn't; he didn't have to, he did it sober."[14]

The trial, which involved hundreds of witnesses, twenty prosecutors, and forty-five defense lawyers, was extensively covered by the international press. As a result of the testimony, the German universities Mengele had attended in Frankfurt and Munich revoked his degrees "because of crimes he committed as a doctor in the concentration camp at Auschwitz." Even though he was absent from the proceedings, Mengele's role in the horrors dashed his hopes of being forgotten.

As Israel delayed its search for Mengele to pursue other priorities, and West Germany concentrated its efforts in Paraguay rather than Brazil, individual Nazi hunters tried to take up the cause. During this period, a number of people were reported by the press as actually having seen the Auschwitz Angel of Death.

Renowned Nazi hunter Simon Wiesenthal claimed that a dozen Auschwitz camp survivors (known as The Committee of Twelve) had banded together to capture Mengele. Supposedly, they just missed kidnapping him in a Paraguyan jungle hotel.[15]

Less dramatic sightings were reported as well. Sonia Tauber, an Auschwitz survivor, claimed that in 1965 Mengele came to shop at a jewelry store she owned in Argentina. The woman described how her heart nearly skipped a beat when she realized that the well-dressed gentleman browsing through her diamond showcase was the same Nazi doctor who had sent so many innocent people to their death with the wave of his hand. Her husband reported how Ms. Tauber had rushed to the back of the shop, and with her face drained of color, uttered, "Mengele, that was Mengele."[16]

As "Mengele sightings" continued to be reported, the myth surrounding the now legendary vil-
lian grew. It was said that anyone who dared to track
Mengele risked his life doing so. Reporters eagerly
sought interviews with members of The Committee
of Twelve or other avengers.

The reported sightings of Mengele made the Brazilian police look inept in their efforts to capture him.
In a vigorous attempt to find him, in May 1966, they
arrested a German traveler near the Paraguay bor-
der. As the Portuguese-speaking police didn't know
very much German, they misinterpreted the man's
pleas to be released as a full confession from the
Nazi war criminal. Unfortunately, before the mistake was realized, the newspapers heralded the
headline that Mengele had finally been captured and
was under arrest. It was the sixth false headline of
Mengele's capture within a five-year period.

Perhaps the most ambitious story regarding Mengele's "capture" came from Erich Erdstein, a former Brazilian police officer. In fact, Erdstein even
claims to have shot and killed the Nazi doctor. Ex-
ploiting his experience as a former Brazilian police
officer who'd been privy to inside information, Erdstein had announced that he was about to kidnap
Mengele. He sold the rights to his story in advance
to a European magazine.

Erdstein explained that his plan was to capture
Mengele on one of the doctor's frequent trips from
Argentina to Paraguay. Supposedly, on the day in
question, gunfire erupted as Erdstein tried to take
Mengele, and he shot Mengele twice, hitting him in
the chest and neck.

The former police officer swore that all this took
place in September 1968, but in October of that year,

(36)

Erdstein abruptly left South America. His reason for fleeing was that after killing Mengele his own life was no longer safe. However, in actuality, Erdstein was wanted by the police for passing bad checks. When confronted by the reality that he hadn't killed Mengele, Erdstein replied, "Well, I must have shot a double then."[17]

Although some of the individuals who claimed they saw Mengele were sincere, it's doubtful that even a few such sightings were authentic. A later compilation of Mengele's diaries, autobiography, and family letters indicates that, due to the high risk factors involved, Mengele never returned to Paraguay after 1960. Unfortunately, the vast majority of sightings pinpoint Mengele in Paraguay past that time. In addition, none of the reported locations coincide with the places where Mengele is actually now known to have been on the given dates.

Meanwhile, Mengele remained on the Stammer farm in a family situation that seemed to grow tenser by the day. Mengele and the Stammers had become mutually dependent. Mengele had purchased a half-interest in their farm, and as a result of his investment, the family's life-style had substantially improved. They'd been able to afford better farm machinery and a new car. Mengele, who had never lived by himself in South America, felt protected within a family setting, where he thought he'd be less likely to be found.

However, Mengele was not an easy houseguest to tolerate. During the thirteen years he stayed with the Stammers, Mengele attempted to dominate and control the family members' lives. He meddled in their financial concerns and criticized the manner in which the Stammers raised their children. Mengele also forbade the Stammers to speak in their native Hungarian language in his presence, because he felt they might be talking about him. As Mrs. Stammer recalled, "Mengele said, 'I forbid it. In my presence, you have to speak German.'"[18]

To worsen the situation, Mr. Stammer, who enjoyed drinking and having a good time, especially resented Mengele's austere and dominating intrusiveness. Often Stammer took pleasure in taunting Mengele. At times, the two men's shouting matches lasted into the night. When reminded that he was merely a guest in their home, Mengele retorted, "I own half of all this, and I will do as I please."[19]

The Stammer children too developed an intense dislike for Mengele, who they felt had no right to attempt to discipline them. Roberto, the Stammers' eldest son, hated the cold, authoritarian, distant man who continually tried to dominate their household. According to the boy's mother, "My son detested him. Peter [Mengele] was always ordering him to do this, do that. My son would say, 'Well, why should I? You're not my father.'"[20]

With the passage of time, the stress generated by the situation only seemed to worsen. According to Mrs. Stammer: "As time passed, he even began to behave as if he were a superior human being. We were far away, isolated, alone—far away from everything and everybody. We waited and things became more complicated because everybody was nervous and tense."[21]

Then, early in 1969, the Stammers decided to sell their farm. Now that both their sons had completed school, they wanted to be closer to where Mr. Stammer had found employment. The family purchased a four-bedroom home on two acres of land on a hillside. Since Mengele provided half the money for the purchase, he could not be left behind.

Once in their new surroundings, Mengele tried to spend more of his time working on the grounds than with the family. He constructed a sturdy fence around the house, which he fortified with a heavy-duty gate and a secure lock.

While Mengele remained in Brazil, he also made the acquaintance of another couple, Wolfram and Liselotte Bossert. Like Mengele, the Bosserts were Austrians, and they shared many of his racial and political views. Upon learning Mengele's true identity, the couple reacted sympathetically. The Bosserts were careful never to betray Mengele to the authorities. Instead, they directed much of their energy toward shielding him. The couple's friendship proved quite beneficial to Mengele. Their assistance became instrumental to his survival when, in 1972, the former Auschwitz doctor became ill.

Throughout the numerous anxiety-filled years of evading his captors, Mengele had developed a nervous habit of biting the ends of his long moustache. After a time, he had ingested enough hair to develop a ball that caused an intestinal blockage. Although he always tried to avoid going into town, Mengele's condition became so painful and serious that he decided to be admitted to the local hospital.

In order to receive medical treatment, Mengele was forced to present an ID card to the hospital's admitting department. The only card available to him at the time was a forgery that had been issued to a forty-seven-year-old man. Mengele was considerably older, and the age discrepancy was noted by

Josef Mengele sits with Liselotte Bossert and the Bossert children. Notice how Mengele turns away from the camera. Most Nazi war criminals hesitated to have their pictures taken at all.

the physician treating him. The doctor was puzzled by this patient who physically seemed so much older than his ID card indicated.

The Bosserts came swiftly to Mengele's aid by concocting a story to fool the hospital personnel. They said that the birth date noted on the ID card was a clerical error that the Brazilian government had promised to correct with the issuance of a new card in the near future.

Although the explanation was barely believable, Mengele's physician declined to question the discrepancy further. If the hospital had delved into the matter more thoroughly, Mengele might have been captured at that point.

Mengele later wrote that the most difficult aspect of his hospital stay was avoiding the temptation to discuss aspects of his ailment with the other physicians. Although he wanted to be involved in planning his course of treatment, the Auschwitz doctor forced himself to remain silent. It was crucial that no one on the hospital staff suspect that he had any real medical knowledge; everyone had to think that Mengele was nothing more than an aging farmer.

Unable to tolerate their often disagreeable houseguest and business partner any longer, the Stammers meanwhile decided to sell their property and move to a new location. Only this time they refused to take Mengele with them, even if it meant returning his investment.

Forced for the first time to live alone while in exile, Mengele became embittered over the Stammers' deliberate rejection of him. As he wrote in his diary: "Again, it is not so much to be alone but to be left in the lurch that hurts so much."[22]

At that point, Mengele had to find another place to stay. Although the Bosserts remained Mengele's faithful friends, they decided against inviting him to live with them. The Bosserts had a very small home. In addition, they had also witnessed the disastrous effect Mengele's presence had had on the Stammer family.

By 1975, Mengele was on his own in Brazil. He used his share of the sale of the Stammer property to buy a small bungalow. His new yellow stucco house was actually little more than a shack. It had a tiny bedroom, an outmoded bathroom, and a small kitchen. Perhaps its best feature was that it was near the Bosserts' home. By then, they were the only individuals who offered Mengele moral support and friendship on a regular basis.

Mengele survived the loss of the Stammer family, but his new life-style left him extremely depressed. As he related in his diary entry for April 7, 1975: "It has a wearing effect on me, to be left so very much isolated and excluded and all alone."[23]

To try to refurbish his run-down bungalow, Mengele painted the bedroom dark green and made some other improvements, but he remained tormented by his isolation. He wrote of his predicament: "My cage becomes more comfortable, but it remains a cage."[24] Mengele also had to contend with increasing financial difficulties. Although his family in Europe continued to contribute to his support, the amount he now received was hardly enough to live comfortably.

Mengele wanted to purchase a record player and tape deck to try to relieve his boredom, but he doubted that he could afford it. He wrote home to his relatives, telling them how, now more than ever, he was dependent on their help. Even the Stammers felt that Mengele's family could have done more to help him in the later years. Mrs. Stammer had often mentioned that Mengele's family hadn't been very generous to him.

While living alone, Mengele's health also began to seriously decline. He suffered from high blood pressure, migraine headaches, rheumatism, a spinal problem, and other ailments. His anxiety over being kidnapped by the Israelis had reached a new height. Once when Mengele ventured out to a local food shop, he decided that another customer there was scrutinizing him too closely. Thinking that perhaps he'd been recognized, Mengele hurriedly left the shop. Fearful for his safety, he never returned there again.

Every day Mengele scoured the local newspapers for articles detailing the various attempts at his capture. These intrigues always greatly distressed Mengele; he wanted more information than could be gleaned from the paper. Mengele would always ask the Bosserts if they thought the article was accurate, or if the authorities or Nazi hunters had planted the story in order to keep him on the run. But he never learned the truth. Instead, he continued to live in fear. At night, Mengele slept with a loaded pistol next to his bed.

As time passed, Mengele's physical health as well as his outlook on life began a downward spiral, and he increasingly spoke of suicide. Then on an afternoon in May 1976, he became quite dizzy and ill. A severe pain had struck the right side of Mengele's head, and he experienced a tingling sensation on the left half of his face and in his left arm. As a physician, it wasn't difficult for Mengele to recognize that he'd had a stroke.

His friend Wolfram Bossert was not surprised by the attack. As he wrote to one of Mengele's associates in Europe: "I am convinced that his stroke was due to an internal damming up because he has no professional life . . . his explosive nature was imposed on the people he lives with. The sudden isolation after ten years of relative security . . . together with the general stress and worry about his existence . . . brought on the stroke."[25]

Despite the fact that Mengele regained full movement in his limbs within days following his stroke, his health continued to be a source of great concern to him. He wrote the following to his family: "I had a bad time of it the last two months. Long-lasting pain of this kind causes one to be very nervous and sick of living."[26]

In February 1979, Mengele agreed to join the Bossert family for a short vacation at the beach. Mengele was so afraid of being recognized that he remained inside the tiny beach house for the first two days of their stay. He kept the shutters tightly drawn in spite of the intense heat, creating an indoor environment that the others described as being something like a steambath.

Finally, on February 7, Mengele emerged from the house for a walk along the beach. It was another steamy day, and the sun blazed down on Mengele as he walked and talked with Bossert. Later in the afternoon, Mengele decided to take a dip in the ocean in order to cool off. It was the last swim Mengele would ever take. While in the ocean, he suffered a second stroke, which paralyzed his body. Despite the efforts of the Bossert family to save him, Mengele drowned.

Since Mengele was buried under a false identity, the search for the Nazi mass murderer continued by those who didn't know that he was actually dead. By 1977, the United States, in conjunction with Israel, had resolved to capture the elusive killer once and for all.

In August 1977, an Argentine magazine reported sightings of Josef Mengele, who had supposedly been driving a large black sedan. Noted Nazi hunter Simon Wiesenthal told *Time* magazine in September 1977 that Mengele divided his time between two luxurious homes, and was continually surrounded by bodyguards at both locations.[27] The effect of the *Time* article was to once again focus the public's attention on the hunt for the Nazi who had extinguished the lives of thousands.

In March 1979, the CBS television show "60 Minutes" broadcast a British documentary on the hunt for Mengele. The program, which was seen by over twenty million viewers, shocked Americans of all ages and ethnic backgrounds. Letters and phone calls to members of Congress poured in. The people demanded that America take action to force Paraguay to relinquish this fugitive from justice. Although Paraguay had gone on record stating that Mengele had long since left its borders, its denial remained unbelieved.

A U.S. senator, Jesse Helms, responded to the public's outcry for Mengele's capture. Senator Helms drafted Senate Resolution number 184, which requested the president to demand that Paraguay apprehend Josef Mengele and extradite him to the Federal Republic of Germany to stand trial. As Senator

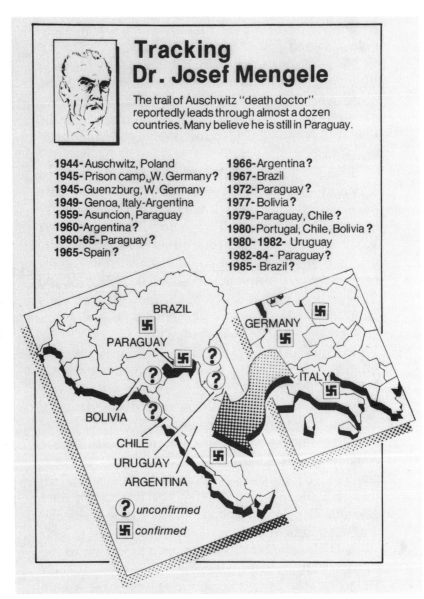

Tracking Dr. Josef Mengele

The trail of Auschwitz "death doctor" reportedly leads through almost a dozen countries. Many believe he is still in Paraguay.

1944- Auschwitz, Poland
1945- Prison camp, W. Germany?
1945- Guenzburg, W. Germany
1949- Genoa, Italy-Argentina
1959- Asuncion, Paraguay
1960- Argentina?
1960-65- Paraguay?
1965- Spain?

1966- Argentina?
1967- Brazil
1972- Paraguay?
1977- Bolivia?
1979- Paraguay, Chile?
1980- Portugal, Chile, Bolivia?
1980-1982- Uruguay
1982-84- Paraguay?
1985- Brazil?

BRAZIL
PARAGUAY
GERMANY
ITALY
BOLIVIA
CHILE
URUGUAY
ARGENTINA

? unconfirmed
confirmed

This map illustrates the path that some believed Mengele might have followed while in hiding. The trail leads through nearly a dozen countries.

Helms described Mengele's legacy in the Senate debate that followed: "The fact that Josef Mengele should remain today in freedom, never having been brought to trial, makes him a living symbol of the Holocaust we cannot continue to tolerate. To forgive or forget the crimes of Josef Mengele would require the amputation of our conscience and the dismemberment of our memory."[28]

The Senate unanimously passed Senator Helms's resolution. In addition, aid to Paraguay was held back and defense cuts were threatened. In response, the Paraguayan government revoked Mengele's citizenship and again truthfully stated that he had left Paraguay a number of years before. However, due to the country's poor record on human rights and its reputation as a haven for fugitives, few people actually believed the government.

Simon Wiesenthal offered a new reward of fifty thousand dollars for Mengele's capture. He also urged the Paraguayan government to issue a new arrest warrant. To create further interest in the case, Wiesenthal offered the Paraguayan police an additional ten thousand dollars for Mengele's arrest.

During this period, the various sightings and reports regarding Mengele's whereabouts continued. In 1981, Mengele was said to be hiding out in an affluent New York suburb. In fact, the *New York Post* headlines read: "Angel of Death in Westchester County." Later, in 1984, there were other rumors that Mengele's family had purchased large tracts of land in Indiana. The search continued, and although of course no one was able to apprehend Mengele, people everywhere continued to believe that he was still alive.

Then on January 27, 1985, a dramatic event underscored the urgent desire to bring Mengele to justice. On the fortieth anniversary of Auschwitz's liberation, a group of camp survivors held a candlelit walk through the former camp. It was a moving event that received worldwide press coverage. Many of the participants had been scarred or disfigured by Mengele's knife or experiments. In addition, the sets of twins who had survived Mengele's horrendous experiments had begun a campaign to awaken the conscience of the world's governments.

In still another attempt to call attention to the injustice of Mengele's not having been brought to trial, a mock trial was staged in Jerusalem by Simon Wiesenthal and several Israelis. The shocking media event jarred the world's consciousness as Mengele's victims attested to his nightmarish deeds on television. More than one hundred survivors testifed regarding Mengele's crimes.

By the end of 1984, the West Germans and other Nazi hunters were of course no closer to finding Mengele alive than they had ever been. Meanwhile, pressure on the United States government to take action against Mengele continued to mount. At America's insistence, West Germany, Israel, and the United States agreed to pool their information on Mengele's possible whereabouts. Everyone involved felt encouraged by the prospect of combining their resources. At the time, the director of the U.S. Office of Special Investigations was quoted as saying: "Yes, I think we'll get him. I'm ninety-nine-percent sure of that."[29] The possibility that Mengele might already be dead was apparently still never given any serious consideration.

A search of the home of one of Mengele's contacts in Germany revealed several old letters from

Mengele bearing Brazilian postmarks. The next step was to actively involve the Brazilian government. The man put in charge of Brazil's renewed search for Mengele was a fifty-three-year-old police chief named Romeo Tuma. Tuma, who already had a reputation as a feared and aggressive investigator, had actively sought out other Nazi fugitives.

Tuma's local investigation led him to the Bosserts' residence. Inside the couple's home, the police chief found a personal memorial to Mengele. It was composed of the Nazi doctor's writings, numerous photographs, and some of Mengele's personal effects.

The West German authorities immediately sent two officers to assist in the investigation. At first, the Bosserts denied their relationship with the Auschwitz murderer. However, after several hours, they admitted the truth and told the Brazilian police where Mengele's body could be found. Mr. Bossert told the investigators: "I didn't think you could find us so quickly."[30]

The Bosserts accompanied the police to the gravesite to make certain the correct coffin was opened. After three hours of digging with picks and shovels, Mengele's grave was finally unearthed. When the lid of his coffin was lifted, Mengele's body was found with his arms placed at his sides instead of crossed over his breast. It seems that this was the traditional SS burial pose.

Mengele's skull was lifted up and held to the light for examination. The remainder of his bones were tossed into a white plastic bag and taken under armed guard to a laboratory for identification.

A team of forensic science experts was assembled to verify Mengele's identity. Their task was es-

Brazilian forensic experts presented facial
reconstructions of Mengele after his remains
were unearthed. The facial reconstruction
on the left shows Mengele at age twenty-eight.
The one on the right shows him at age sixty-eight.
In the middle is the skull of Mengele, the man who
came to be known as the "Angel of Death."

pecially difficult since dental X rays, which are often vital in identifying skeletons, were not available. The forensic scientists tried to see how Mengele's photographs and his known physical characteristics compared with his remains.

The intensive study by the team revealed that the skeleton dug up in Brazil was indeed that of Josef Mengele. On June 21, 1985, the Nazi murderer's skull and bones were placed on exhibit at Brazilian police headquarters for eager onlookers to gaze at. The forensic scientists were present to display their findings and explain how they arrived at their conclusions.

It is ironic that in the end, Mengele's remains were the object of a scientific study. The inhumane doctor whose pseudoscientific endeavors had resulted in annihilation for so many others was finally dead in the eyes of the world and on exhibit for the world's verification.

2

ADOLF EICHMANN

Adolf Eichmann was a creature of habit. For the most part, the once high-ranking Nazi official rigidly adhered to the same daily routine. Now, in 1960, Eichmann resided in San Fernando, a rather drab suburb of Buenos Aires. Though guilty of grievous war crimes and pursued as one of the world's most wanted war criminals, Eichmann had eluded capture and lived in hiding for the past fifteen years. Using the alias Ricardo Klement, he had modestly resided with his wife and three of their four sons in a mud-colored brick house that lacked running water.

Most mornings Eichmann rose early and spent a bit of time puttering around his home. Then he'd wash, shave, dress, and sit down to a hearty German-style breakfast. At about a quarter to seven, Eichmann would leave his home to walk to a nearby bus stop. The local bus took him to his job at a Mercedes-Benz factory in a nearby town. When he arrived at work, he'd punch a time card bearing the name Ricardo Klement and then begin his work in the automobile factory.

Eichmann usually went to lunch at twelve-thirty. He would walk several blocks to a nearby luncheonette, where he would order a modest meal. He would finish eating by about one-thirty, and within half an hour was back at work. At five-thirty, he'd leave work and usually walk straight to the bus stop, where he'd catch the bus to go home.

Although Eichmann was unaware of it, he had been under surveillance by a team of Israeli agents, whose goal it was to capture and bring him to trial in their country. Adolf Eichmann was a much desired target among Nazi hunters. His role in the Nazi party during World War II was singularly significant for its effect on European Jewry: Eichmann had been instrumental in engineering the extermination of the nearly six million Jews who died in the Holocaust.

The team of young Israeli men assigned the task of kidnapping Eichmann had kept a close watch over Ricardo Klement for several weeks. They believed that Ricardo Klement was the fugitive Nazi war criminal Adolf Eichmann, but they couldn't be certain. And it was imperative that they target the correct person, since a mistaken attempt might send the real Adolf Eichmann even deeper under cover.

There was substantial evidence to suggest that Klement was actually Eichmann. For one thing, Klement was supposedly the second husband of Adolf Eichmann's first wife. The two were living together in the Buenos Aires suburb along with three boys who were definitely Adolf Eichmann's sons. The boys had even retained their father's last name. The problem confronting the Israeli agents was the possibility that Ricardo Klement was actually who his wife claimed he was—the man who married Mrs.

Eichmann after her first husband's death and acted as her children's stepfather.

Part of the Israelis' problem had to do with the fact that during the Nazi regime, Adolf Eichmann had made a concerted effort to remain a somewhat shadowy figure. He had avoided cameras whenever possible, and the personal details of his life were contained only within his confidential file at Nazi SS headquarters.

Fortunately, Israeli agents had secured that file. They knew Eichmann's height, hair and eye color, and shoe and collar size, as well as the dates of his promotion, his marriage, and the birth of his children. The height and eye color of the man known as Ricardo Klement appeared to be the same as Eichmann's.

The Israelis were also in possession of a photograph of Eichmann taken in the late 1930s that was located in 1946. Many changes might have taken place over the years to alter Eichmann's appearance. Surely his face would have aged, and it might have been further changed by plastic surgery. It wasn't known whether Eichmann had resorted to plastic surgery, as so many other Nazi fugitives had.

Using hidden cameras, the Israelis had managed to photograph the man known as Ricardo Klement a number of times during their surveillance operations. Since these shots had to be taken at awkward angles in split seconds, the results were hardly perfect portraits.

One snapshot did catch a full-faced view of Eichmann. Although the man in the photo taken by the Israeli agent in 1960 somewhat resembled the one in the 1930s picture, the agents couldn't be certain.

On Monday, March 21, 1960, Ricardo Klement

offered his would-be captors the break they'd been waiting for. That evening when he left work, Klement didn't head directly for the bus stop. Instead, he first stopped at a nearby florist. He left the shop carrying a beautiful bouquet, and proceeded to the bus stop to resume his usual trip home.

The agents wondered what had prompted Klement's purchase of the flowers. Then they realized what day it was. It was Adolf Eichmann's wedding anniversary! It was the extra measure of proof the agents had been waiting for. There was no longer any doubt in their minds that Ricardo Klement and Adolf Eichmann were the same man.

The capture and trial of Adolf Eichmann would perhaps be among the finest hours in the history of justice. At last, one of the most ruthless Nazi perpetrators would have to account to a court of law for his barbarous deeds. Adolf Eichmann had attempted to wipe Jews off the face of the earth for no other reason than that they were members of a religious and ethnic group that the Nazis despised.

Following World War II, a number of war criminals had been tried for their deeds at a tribunal in Nuremberg, Germany. Although Eichmann was in hiding at the time and could not be tried, his name, like that of Dr. Mengele, came up repeatedly in the testimony given. Evidence heard at the Nuremberg Tribunal described Eichmann as being largely responsible for hideous crimes against humanity on a broad scale in over sixteen countries.

When the war was over, Eichmann, along with a number of other Nazi criminals, had good reason to fear for his life. He had heard countless rumors and tales of high-ranking Nazis in hiding who had been pursued and brought to justice. In a number of instances, these men had been ferreted out following long spells in hiding.

Thinking it safer to hide outside of Germany, some Nazi leaders had sought refuge in faraway lands. Many tried to start new lives in the Arab countries of the Middle East. The Arabs were sympathetic to Nazis, and often offered them prestigious jobs at lavish salaries. Eichmann was tempted by this prospect. He'd be able to live freely and in style with his wife and children in a country that shared his intense anti-Jewish sentiments. In an Arab nation, Nazis were not made to feel ashamed of their past. Eichmann would be able to take pride in his sinister accomplishments.

Although Adolf Eichmann had been tempted to take refuge in the Middle East, he decided that the area was potentially too explosive. Since 1948, when the state of Israel came into existence, tensions in the Middle East had risen. Eichmann didn't feel he could remain anonymous in an Arab country, even if he wished to. Living so close to the new Jewish state, he feared he might be an easy target for daring Israeli agents. And if fighting broke out between Israel and the country in which he had sought asylum, Eichmann might find himself no safer than if he had remained in Germany.

Eichmann decided that it was too risky to be that close to the Israelis. Instead, he looked toward South America as a refuge. Life in South America would be more difficult. Instead of a high-paying government position, he'd face poverty and hardship. As anonymity would be vital to his safety, Eichmann would have to live under an assumed identity.

However, there were advantages to hiding out in South America. A number of Nazi party members as well as Germans sympathetic to their ideology were already living there. Staying in a community where there were other Germans might help to take the spotlight off Eichmann, and he was anxious to put thousands of miles between himself and his pursuers.

Another reason why Eichmann had looked to either the Middle East or South America was because he was aware of several underground Nazi organizations that had forged escape routes to these areas for fugitives. Among these was a group known as ODESSA, whose name stood for Organisation der SS Angehörige, or the Organization of Members of the SS. ODESSA's function was to safely guide SS men out of Germany. Like other such organizations, ODESSA had agents in Germany, Austria, Switzerland, and Italy. From Italy, they could arrange safe passage to either the Middle East or South America.

Adolf Eichmann had contacted ODESSA for help early in 1950. By spring of that year, they had guided his passage through Austria to Italy. A priest in Genoa, Italy, sympathetic to the Nazis, secretly worked with ODESSA and other organizations to help Nazi war criminals flee from Europe. Eichmann was given the address of a Franciscan friar who offered him accommodations while in Italy, and later provided the SS leader with a fraudulent refugee passport under the name of Richard Klement.

By June, Eichmann had secured the new passport, and within days an Argentine visa had been obtained for him as well. By the end of the month, he was on board a ship heading for Buenos Aires.

Far away from Germany, in the warm and sunny climate of South America, Eichmann thought he might have finally managed to put thousands of miles between himself and his past. During Eichmann's first months in Argentina, he kept very much to himself. He was friendly only with members of Argentina's Nazi German community, whom he could count on to keep his identity secret. These individuals proved to be quite useful to Eichmann in that they helped him to obtain his Argentine papers as well as to secure employment.

Within two years following his arrival in Argentina, Eichmann was able to send for his wife and children. Mrs. Eichmann, who had told friends and acquaintances that her husband was dead, simply announced that she now intended to marry a close friend from Argentina by the name of Ricardo Klement. Three years later, a fourth son was born to the Eichmanns. They named him Ricardo Francisco after the Genoan priest who'd been so helpful to Eichmann. The child's last name was registered as Klement.

By 1960, the family was living in a one-story brick house in San Fernando. Although their dwelling was run down and offered none of the amenities of gracious living, it suited Eichmann's needs well. The rent was reasonable, and the house was located in a desolate area. The Eichmanns didn't have to live within a complex with other families. No one questioned the barred windows and heavy front door, or the shutters and blinds that always remained tightly drawn.

Eichmann and his family lived quietly, hoping to evade justice, but his pursuers had not given up the chase. By the summer of 1959, Israeli agents had received a tip that Eichmann was living in Argentina using the name Ricardo Klement. The tip came from a South American Jew whose entire family had been gassed in a concentration camp. As this man was not generally known as a Jew, he had managed to become friendly with several members of the German colony in Argentina. From them he had learned that Adolf Eichmann's widow had married a man named Ricardo Klement who worked at the Mercedes-Benz factory. Although he couldn't be sure, the Jewish man thought that perhaps Ricardo Klement was actually Adolf Eichmann. He informed Israeli officials of his hunch, and the Klement family was put under surveillance.

By May 11, 1960, the date of the kidnapping, the Israeli agents knew Eichmann's daily movements by heart. After Eichmann left the evening bus to return to his home, an Israeli agent grabbed him from behind. Eichmann kicked and screamed as he struggled to escape. But he lived, by choice, in a deserted area, and his cries went unheard. The Israeli, with the help of two other agents, forced Eichmann into a waiting car, and they quickly left the area. One of the agents had reached into Eichmann's coat pocket to grab what he thought was a gun. It turned out to be only a flashlight Eichmann would use after leaving the bus each night.

The agents took Eichmann to a "safe house," where he'd be guarded until they were ready to leave the country. As soon as they arrived, Eichmann was stripped and searched to see if he was carrying anything lethal that could be used in a suicide attempt. Even his teeth were examined in the event that a poison vial had been screwed into any of them. It was during the dental examination that Eichmann spoke to his captors for the first time. He simply said, "After fifteen years, don't expect me to be alert. There's nothing in my teeth."[1]

When asked his name, the prisoner answered without hesitation, "I am Adolf Eichmann."[2] Then a moment later he added, "I know that I am in the hands of Israelis." The agents were startled. Not a word of Hebrew had been spoken in his presence. But Eichmann had guessed the truth. After fifteen years of hiding, the chase had finally ended.

After a careful inspection, Eichmann's clothes were returned to him. He was served adequate meals, but was given only a spoon to eat with. Eichmann was allowed to sleep whenever he wished, but his captors kept a light on at all times. They took turns guarding him throughout the day and night, making certain that Eichmann was never left unattended.

On the evening on which the group was to begin their trip back to Israel, Eichmann was given coffee that had been drugged. In less than an hour, he was fast asleep. The agents dressed Eichmann in a dressing gown, as they hoped to board him onto an airplane under the guise of being an extremely ill traveler.

While Eichmann was still heavily sedated, he was carried onto the plane on a stretcher. Two Israeli agents who walked at his side posed as male nurses responsible for his care. A third agent, at the stretcher's rear, was supposedly a worried relative.

The seats on the plane had been arranged to accommodate a sleeping patient. Before arriving in Israel, the plane had to stop in West Africa to refuel. The entire trip went smoothly. Eichmann slept through nearly the whole journey. Whenever the drowsiness seemed to wear off, one of the agents offered him another cup of drugged coffee.

When the plane arrived in Israel, an ambulance was driven up to the runway to transport Eichmann to his place of confinement. For added security, several police cars followed the ambulance to its destination.

At four o'clock that afternoon, the prime minister of Israel issued an important statement to the country's governing body. In a clear voice, Prime Minister David Ben-Gurion announced,

> A short time ago, one of the greatest Nazi war criminals, Adolf Eichmann, who was responsible, together with Nazi leaders, for what they called the "final solution of the Jewish question"—that is, the extermination of six million Jews of Europe—was found . . . is already under arrest in Israel and will shortly be put on trial under the Nazis and Nazi Collaborators Law.[3]

Ben-Gurion's statement was met with an overwhelming round of applause. One of the principal murderers of the Jewish people was now in Israel awaiting trial. Adolf Eichmann had been brought to justice.

THE EICHMANN TRIAL

On Tuesday morning, April 11, 1961, Adolf Eichmann went on trial for his life. By now it had become clear that the Israelis were determined to give Eichmann a fair trial and to have the world recognize it as such. Normally, only an attorney who has passed the Israeli bar exam can try a case in an Israeli court. However, this requirement was waived in the Eichmann case, and he was permitted to have the attorney of his choice.

Adolf Eichmann chose a German attorney named Dr. Robert Servatius to defend him. Dr. Servatius insisted on bringing along an assistant defense counsel from Germany, as well as substantial German secretarial help. The Israeli government agreed to his requests. Dr. Servatius also wished to address the court in German, and to receive a German translation of everything said in the courtroom in Hebrew. The Israelis went along with his demands.

A few months later, Eichmann's defense attorney informed the Israeli government that Eichmann was actually unable to afford an attorney. He asked that the Israelis instead pay his costly fees. Many people were angered by what they viewed as an outrageous and insulting demand. Knowing Eichmann's family in Germany to be financially successful, they wondered if his relatives and friends in Europe couldn't raise the money for his defense. There had also been rumors that Eichmann's wife and sons had received considerable sums from the publication of his memoirs. However, Eichmann's defense attorney assured the Israeli government that no funds were forthcoming from these sources and that if he weren't promptly paid he would withdraw from the case.

The Israelis felt that they couldn't prove that Eichmann had been given a fair trial if he were denied the attorney he wished to represent him. Some people felt that Israel's commitment to allow Eichmann the attorney of his choice was being exploited through this demand for money. Nevertheless, because the Israelis were determined to try Eichmann by due process of law, there was little choice left in the matter.

Distasteful to them as it was, the Israeli government paid Dr. Servatius thirty thousand dollars for trying the case. Because of their commitment to a democratic process, Israeli taxpayers had to pay the legal fees of the man charged with murdering many of their family members.

Although Eichmann did not appear stubborn or aggressive during the trial, prosecutors found it difficult to pry direct answers out of him. When questioned about documents in which he was mentioned or orders having his signature, he continually insisted that he either knew nothing about them or could not remember his role in these actions. Hoping to avoid the death penalty for his deeds, Eichmann tried to be evasive. And since the Israeli government had been so accommodating to his needs so far, he hoped to be successful.

The sensational Eichmann trial had drawn press from around the globe. On the opening day of the trial, three hundred and seventy-six visiting correspondents from fifty countries were present in the courtroom. Four television cameras were also focused on the proceedings. The curious were eager to see how this very ordinary, mild-looking, and balding man who wore thick-rimmed glasses could have committed some of the most hideous crimes imaginable.

As the Israeli prosecutor's opening statement indicated:

> When I stand before you, O Judges of Israel, to lead the prosecution of Adolf Eichmann, I do not stand alone. With me here are six million accusers. But they cannot

*The Jerusalem courtroom in which a three-man
Israeli tribunal sentenced former Gestapo officer
Adolf Eichmann to death. Eichmann stands in
the bulletproof glass booth at the left.*

rise to their feet and point their finger at the man in the dock with the cry *"J'accuse"* on their lips. For they are now only ashes—ashes piled high on the hills of Auschwitz and the fields of Treblinka and strewn in the forests of Poland. Their graves are scattered throughout Europe. Their blood cries out, but their voice is stilled. Therefore will I be their spokesman. In their name I will unfold this terrible indictment.[4]

The man on trial was a new kind of murderer. He was not a man who'd made a grievous error in a moment of rage, but rather someone who, with decided ease and methodical planning, had ordered and directed the murder of millions of innocent individuals. Eichmann was, the prosecutor went on to state,

the kind [of killer] that exercises his bloody craft behind a desk, and only occasionally does the deed with his own hands. . . . But it was his word that put gas chambers into action; he lifted the telephone, and railway trains left for the extermination centers; his signature it was that sealed the doom of tens of thousands. He had but to give the order, and troopers took off to rout Jews out of their homes, to beat and torture them and drive them into ghettos, to steal their property and, after brutality and pillage, after all had been wrung from them, when even their hair had been taken, to transport them en masse to their slaughter. Even their dead bodies were not immune. Gold teeth were extracted and wedding rings torn from fingers.[5]

The prosecution identified Eichmann as "the one who planned, initiated, and organized"[6] the actions. On his word, millions of people were put to death, not for any crime, but simply because they were Jews.

Adolf Eichmann's trial meant a great deal to

Jews throughout the world as well as in the state of Israel. While it is true that the Nazis murdered millions of other innocent people such as Gypsies, homosexuals, the mentally retarded, individuals who disagreed with their policies, and scores of others, Eichmann had taken a special personal interest in the Jews.

The prosecutor defined Eichmann's role in Hitler's plan as follows:

> There was only one man who had been concerned almost entirely with the Jews, whose business had been their destruction, whose role in the establishment of the iniquitous regime had been limited to them. That man was Adolf Eichmann. . . . The mission of the accused, in which for years he saw his destiny and calling, and to which he devoted himself with enthusiasm and endless zeal, was the destruction of the Jews.[7]

Eichmann had been formally sworn into the SS in November 1932. Six years later, on November 9, 1938, what was known as Kristallnacht ("The Night of Broken Glass") came to pass. That night, Nazis burned one hundred and ninety-one synagogues (Jewish houses of worship), and completely demolished another seventy-six. As the flames blazed, Nazi thugs broke into Jewish homes, shops, and businesses to loot, plunder, and destroy. That night, thousands of Jews were rounded up and sent off to concentration camps. Nazi officials said that this was essential in order "to protect the Jews from the wrath of the people."[8]

Kristallnacht initiated a new phase in the Nazi's treatment of Jews. They now felt they could proceed more rapidly with their plans for "the final solution of the Jewish problem."

It was at this point that Eichmann's role in the Holocaust came into full play. It was Eichmann who issued detailed directions for the deportations to Auschwitz as well as ordered supplies of the gas used to kill Jews. He also worked closely with representatives of satellite governments to encourage them to implement strategies against their Jewish citizens.

In the early stages of the mass killings, Eichmann visited the camps, where he inspected the extermination systems to ensure that they were operating at optimum efficiency. Eichmann also oversaw the methods employed in the mass shootings of Jews. As he watched the naked bodies of men, women, and children fall into the previously prepared mass graves, he remarked that the "blood spurted from the grave as if from a spring."[9]

Eichmann also expressed concern that the Jews were not being killed at a sufficiently rapid pace. Wishing to liquidate vast numbers of human beings, he hastened the creation of gas chambers and crematoria at the extermination centers. Once satisfied that the murders had been speeded up, Eichmann stepped up the number of transports carrying people to the camps.

This young man is about to sweep away the broken glass of shop windows in Berlin on November 10, 1938. The previous night the Nazis had demolished thousands of Jewish facilities in what later came to be known as Kristallnacht, or "the Night of Broken Glass."

In fact, Eichmann's office issued the instructions containing the departure time and serial number of each train as well as the route taken to the camp of destination. In turn, the various camps reported regularly to Eichmann's office, furnishing him with timely reports of the number of victims who had arrived and been processed through the gas chambers.

It is ironic that a man largely responsible for a mass execution program that extended across the European continent should be as attentive to small details as Adolf Eichmann was. Eichmann wanted to be kept informed of the exact departure times of the various trains. When it came to his attention that a particular train had been late, it was not uncommon for him to explode into a furious rage.

Eichmann took a comparable interest in the minute details of the cases involving individual Jews. He had grown obsessed with the goal that no one should escape. Whenever it came to his attention that a particular Jew had been shown special consideration that might ensure that individual's safety, he was quick to react.

For example, in 1943, Eichmann heard that a prominent Romanian Jew had been making arrangements to secure passage out of the country. At this point, Romania was still not under German rule, although the country had already been pressured by Germany in various ways. On June 2, 1943, Eich-

Row after row of bodies of slain prisoners lie on the pavement of a German concentration camp.

mann wrote to the SS officer in charge there, stating, "Please use all means at your disposal to prevent the emigration of the Jew Max Auschnitt, living in Bucharest, and arrange for his inclusion in the general measures being taken against the Jews." To ensure that his wishes would be respected, Eichmann added, "I expect to be kept informed of what is being done."[10]

On another occasion, it came to Eichmann's attention that a Jewish man named Golub, who had been imprisoned in the Drancy camp in France, was about to be granted citizenship by a Latin American country. If the proper papers came through, this would allow Mr. Golub to emigrate to South America. In order to prevent Golub from escaping death at the Nazis' hands, Eichmann cabled Gestapo headquarters in Paris with orders that Golub be immediately dispatched to Auschwitz for extermination.

In a number of instances, the German Foreign Ministry urged Eichmann to save individual Jews for diplomatic reasons. One such case involved the senior French officer Robert Masse. Masse had been captured during battle, but had nevertheless been imprisoned in a concentration camp because he was Jewish. As usual, Eichmann refused, offering the Foreign Ministry what had become his common reply, "For reasons of principle, the request cannot be granted."[11]

At one point, the Swedish government tried to interfere with Eichmann's plans in a small way. Hoping to save thirty Norwegian Jews who had been born in Sweden, the government granted them Swedish citizenship and asked that they be sent to Sweden. As the Swedish representative stated to the Gestapo in Oslo, "They too are human, those unfortunates." The request was sent to Eichmann for his consideration. His reply was, "The efforts [of the Swedish government] should be frustrated, and I intend to include those Jews as soon as possible within the framework of general Jewish activities."[12]

The list of these incidents involving Adolf Eichmann seems endless. The portrait of the man that emerges is that of a cold-blooded killer who was almost methodical in his cunning and calculated cruelties.

Adolf Eichmann's trial in Israel lasted a little over eight months. On Friday, December 15, 1961, Eichmann was brought into the courtroom for the verdict. He stood with his thighs braced against the table as the judge began to read the verdict. The court found Adolf Eichmann guilty of participating in "crimes of horror unparalleled in their nature and scope. The purpose of these crimes, of which the accused has been found guilty, was to wipe out the entire Jewish people from the face of the earth."[13] The judge concluded his delivery by sentencing Eichmann to death: "This court sentences Adolf Eichmann to death for his guilt in committing crimes against the Jewish people, crimes against humanity and war crimes."[14]

Prior to being hanged, Eichmann was visited by the Reverend William Hull, a Protestant clergyman. The minister had been assigned by the Israeli government to assist Eichmann with his spiritual needs prior to his death. Reverend Hull encouraged Eichmann to repent and to return to the Church. However, even within an hour of his execution, Eichmann told him, "I am not prepared to discuss the Bible. I do not have time to waste."[15]

Once on the gallows, Eichmann declined the use of a black hood. His last words before the noose was placed around his neck were, "Long live Germany. Long live Argentina. Long live Austria. These are the countries with which I have been most closely associated, and I shall not forget them. I greet my wife, my family and my friends. I had to obey the rules of war and my flag."[16] Three hours after the execution, Eichmann's body was cremated. His ashes were collected in a plain metal jar. The Israelis had decided to follow the precedent set by the trial of Nazi war criminals at Nuremberg, in which the ashes of the condemned were scattered at sea.

The urn containing Eichmann's ashes was placed on a special police patrol boat. Although Reverend Hull was present on the boat, he did not conduct funeral rites, as Eichmann had so firmly refused to return to the Church. The clergyman was later to describe Adolf Eichmann as having been "the hardest man I ever saw."[17]

Eichmann's ashes were scattered over the Mediterranean Sea. So ended the life of a man who'd been instrumental in the murder of millions.

3

AN UNSAVORY ASSORTMENT

Throughout World War II, Allied forces had marveled at advanced German technology. It was well known in the military and political circles of the Allied powers that brilliant scientists were employing their extraordinary expertise to achieve Hitler's aims. Indeed, captured German equipment confirmed the Allies' worst fears. For example, while the barrel of an American-made 50-caliber machine gun eroded after eight hundred rounds, comparable German models lasted for five thousand. German hollow-charge heavy rockets and high-performance antitank equipment far surpassed comparable American equipment.

Germany had been the first country to develop jet fighters. They also appeared to be far ahead of Allied efforts in developing long-range rocketing and radio-guidance systems. Because German rockets were powered by liquid rather than solid fuel, they were significantly lighter in weight. German scientists had developed pilotless aircraft that were known as flying bombs. In addition to numerous other scientific advances, the Germans had also perfected aircraft guns fired by electricity, infrared receivers with the ability to detect aircraft exhaust fumes from a distance of sixteen thousand yards, and a poisonous nerve gas.[1]

It became clear to the Allies that the spoils of World War II would include looting Germany's military technology as well as securing the services of the brilliant scientific minds who developed it.

According to George Szamuelyin in his article "Did the U.S. Recruit Nazi War Criminals?",

> The looting of German military technology began during the war itself. By July 1944, the Russians had cleaned out Blizna missile center. The French grabbed the aircraft factories and denied access to them to the British and the Americans. The British seized the submarine and torpedo plant at Kiel. The Russians extracted all the secrets they needed to build up their postwar submarine force from the torpedo research center at Gydnia, in Poland.[2]

Many people believe that the greatest scientific spoils of World War II fell into American hands. U.S. Army troops were the first to arrive at the Mittelwerk underground rocket factory near Nordhausen. It was there that the German V-2 rockets that had devastated London were being manufactured.

Along with the equipment, arriving American troops found outstanding German scientists waiting for them at the facility. Such men as Wernher von Braun, Walter Dornberger, Arthur Rudolph, and a number of others enthusiastically surrendered to the American forces. The scientists told the conquering Americans that they had fourteen tons of documents containing research data hidden away. They tried to stress to the Americans that they weren't Nazis, but in fact had only been scientists used by Hitler's regime. The men said that they were eager to emigrate to America and begin doing research to advance the United States' position as a world power.

Gaining their expertise would certainly be a boost to America's developing technology, but there were serious obstacles in the way. For one thing, the conditions at the Mittelwerk factory where the scientists had conducted their research and work were appalling. The gigantic tunnels used, which had been built without the assistance of power drills or other mechanical tools, had been dug by slave labor. At first, the laborers were brought in from the Buchenwald concentration camp. Later a new slave camp, Dora, was established primarily to meet Mittelwerk's manpower needs. Driven by cruel and inhumane SS guards, the slave laborers died by the thousands while completing this awesome task.

As Tom Bowker described the conditions in his book *The Paperclip Conspiracy*:

> At least twenty thousand men would die there before the end of the war. Working without power drills or mechanical excavators, the slaves were constantly threatened and beaten while they dug, hammered and heaved their pickaxes. Despite the constant arrival of new labor, the number of workers never increased. On the average, one hundred men a day died of exhaustion, starvation, and disease, or were murdered by SS guards, either on a whim or as punishment.
>
> Their emaciated bodies were usually disposed of in the crematoria at nearby Camp Dora; those who were hanged as punishment were left at the end of the rope

for days, successfully intimidating the survivors. Replacements supplied by the SS from other concentration camps arrived on demand from Rudolph or Wernher von Braun [head scientists].[3]

Survivors who worked at the factory have attested that although SS officers controlled the work force, the SS acted only on the authority of the scientists in charge. Joint meetings on how to boost the workload and daily production involved both groups. In addition, workers suspected of sabotage were singled out to the SS by the scientists, since they were the only individuals on the premises who were sufficiently knowledgeable to detect willful acts of destruction.

One survivor described how workers suspected of sabotage or other infractions of behavior were dealt with: "On one occasion fifty-seven men were [hanged]. An electric crane in the tunnel lifted twelve prisoners at a time, hands behind their backs, a piece of wood in their mouths, hanged by a length of wire attached at the back of their necks to prevent them from crying out."[4] The others would be taken from their duties momentarily to witness the executions and then returned to their places in the tunnels to continue the rocket assembly.

Another survivor, French resistance hero Yves Beon, recalled that those hanged "would be left for days afterward dangling from the rope, their trousers fallen on the ground below mixed with excreta, while the German civilians [scientists] just passed by without looking, without any sign of emotion."[5]

One of the better-known scientists, Arthur Rudolph, had at one time been seen marching through the streets of Berlin singing the Nazi party's song,

"Horst Wessel Lied," which contains the lyrics "When Jewish blood spurts from the knife, then all goes twice as well." For the most part, Rudolph directed the full-scale production at Mittelwerk.

Despite the ugliness and inhumanity that shrouded the German scientists' accomplishments, some influential U.S. military intelligence personnel wanted to have the captured scientists continue their work in the United States. The military feared the loss of the outstanding scientists to other countries, such as France and the Soviet Union, who didn't appear to have any qualms about benefiting from the work of the Nazis. There were rumors that French agents had kidnapped the wives and children of some of the German experts and had refused to release them or guarantee their safety unless their husbands returned to work in the French zone.

The Soviets, on their part, attempted to lure the German scientists with generous inducements. The Russians offered them high salaries as well as comfortable villas, free household servants, and an ample supply of food, cigarettes, and clothing for themselves and their families.

In response to these circumstances, the U.S. Joint Intelligence Committee issued a grim forecast for America's future: "Unless the migration of important German scientists and technicians into the Soviet zone is immediately stopped, we believe that the Soviet Union within a relatively short time may equal United States' developments in the fields of atomic research and guided missiles."[6]

However, serious moral problems marred the entry of German scientists into the United States. Many of the scientists had been as brutal as they were brilliant. An overwhelming number of them had been members of the Nazi party. Some had even belonged to the SS. Such backgrounds made them ineligible for entry into this country.

However, it became increasingly difficult for the U.S. military to watch the German scientific geniuses being siphoned off to competing foreign powers. A good deal of pressure was placed on the U.S. government to make some concessions to remedy the situation.

On March 4, 1946, the State-War-Navy Coordinating Committee issued a policy statement that somewhat enlarged the entryway to America's scientific community. The revised policy permitted the entry of outstanding scientists into the United States provided that their presence here was in the country's "national interest" and that none of the scientists had been "active Nazis" or otherwise objectionable.

In many instances, it had been up to the American officials in charge to determine exactly what being an "active Nazi" meant. Individuals with cloudy pasts were sometimes viewed as being somewhat less at blame if their skills were badly needed.

For example, some of the researchers at Mittelwerk assured the American investigators that although they knew that the working conditions of the slave laborers at the plant were deplorable, there was really nothing they could do to change things. They claimed that it was the SS rather than they who dealt with the workers and sanctioned the horrendous scheduling procedures which cost men their lives.

Time and time again, the researchers stressed that they were strictly "professionals" who concerned themselves only with scientific advances.

Some stated that they generally made a point of not inquiring about how their directives affected the conditions under which the laborers worked.

However, although they might not have placed a noose around an inmate's neck, it can be argued that, at the very least, they could have refused to work at a facility where such conditions existed. Certainly, their unusual brilliance and expertise in their fields afforded them some degree of power and influence.

Still, even in cases where the desired individuals failed to meet the U.S. government's more liberal criteria, the military found loopholes in the policy by offering the people only short-term contracts and denying their families the right to emigrate. It was determined that the scientists offered contracts to work in the United States would be identified by having paper clips attached to their files. That was the birth of what became known as Project Paperclip.

To facilitate Project Paperclip, still other measures were instituted. Ensuring that the U.S. did not miss out on its opportunity to garner a good share of the talent, on September 3, 1946, the State Department issued a new directive which allowed the entry of a thousand scientists and refused admission only to those in the "automatic arrest category through the denazification program of the U.S. government." This meant that a brilliant scientist could be admitted to the United States provided that he was not a wanted war criminal.

In determining which scientists were to be recruited by the United States, military officials continually had to evaluate individual situations and circumstances. Although outright war criminals were not actively sought to promote America's interests, as time passed, American military officials appeared to become more lax in deciding who would come over.

According to George Szamuelyin in *Commentary*:

> Herbertus Strughold, who as director of Hitler's air ministry research institute had known about human experiments conducted at Dachau and elsewhere, was brought to conduct research into space medicine. Kurt Blome, who had been acquitted at Nuremberg of conducting human experiments, was hired by the U.S. Chemical Corporation to perform research for biological warfare. Then there was Walter Schreiber, who had been head of the Department of Science and Health in the German High Command and was alleged to have witnessed human experiments. [Blome and Schreiber had to leave as a result of protest].[7]

In order to be certain that the Project Paperclip scientists received visas, U.S. military intelligence had to assure the State Department that these men were not war criminals, as might be assumed by their recorded past actions. To do so, security data and reports compiled by the Joint Intelligence Objectives Agency (JIOA) tended to play down such factors as SS or Nazi party membership. They argued that it was not genuine sentiment, but rather political opportunism and the prospect of professional survival in a Nazi regime that led the scientists to become affiliated with these groups.

Regardless of the various excuses offered, it can be argued that there was at least some distortion involved in paving the way for these scientists to work in the United States. In all such dealings and transactions, the U.S. government was well aware of the fact that scientists turned away could easily find a place for themselves in the Soviet Union. As a result, in many instances, officials were quick to look the other way, and hundreds of German scientists arrived in the United States. Some of these had invalid visas; some had no visas at all.

Army records indicate that by the time Project Paperclip came to a close, on September 30, 1947, the United States had secured four hundred and fifty-seven German scientists. The Soviet Union, on the other hand, gained more than twice that number in all. That meant that out of an estimated twenty-five hundred aeronautic experts available in Germany as of 1945, twenty-five percent went to work for the Soviet Union—either having readily offered their services to the Russians or having been kidnapped by them—eight percent went to France, and twelve percent to the United States.[8] Once things had settled somewhat and the men were actively working on U.S. defense projects, the State Department eventually issued valid visas to all the Paperclip scientists by the summer of 1948.

The end result was that many scientists who had been classified in Germany as "ardent Nazis" were selected to become "model" American citizens following Hitler's defeat. In order to obtain the services of those talented men, U.S. officials too often had to whitewash their unsavory pasts. At times, American officials had engaged in various forms of subterfuge, such as deliberately providing misinformation. In their determination that the United States should match or exceed the Soviet Union in any future conflict, they pursued their unsavory craft with patriotic zeal.

(83)

And the Korean War, on a limited scale, proved to be just such a conflict. Although, unlike the United States, the Soviets did not participate directly in the war, they did provide the communist side with essential military equipment, including jet aircraft. As Tom Bowker puts it:

> The Korean War can be viewed, on a technical level, as a trial of strength between two different teams of Germans: those hired by Americans and those hired by the Soviet Union. The aerial dogfights between Soviet-MIG-15s and the American F-86 Sabres—both designed by German engineers—dispelled for many their doubts about the expediency of plundering Germany's scientific expertise.[9]

It cannot be denied that in the years to come, Project Paperclip scientists rewarded the nation that had given them sanctuary with ample scientific breakthroughs. For example, when America became the first nation to land on the moon in 1969, much of the credit was owed to two groups of imported German scientists. One was Wernher von Braun's rocket team, which had approved the brutal and inhumane use of slave labor at Mittelwerk. The other was a team of German aviation doctors whose outstanding work largely relied on fatal tests performed on inmates at the Dachau concentration camp.

In addition to Project Paperclip, there have been numerous incidents in which individuals with questionable backgrounds entered the United States following World War II.

Charles Allen, Jr., one of the most widely respected authorities on Nazi war criminals in the United States, has cited details involving over one hundred cases in which the United States government in some way utilized individuals who'd been accused of being Nazi war criminals.[10] "Utilizing" these people included such diverse activities as having contact with them, offering them employment, or helping them to obtain entrance visas into the United States.

Among those cited by Allen was Dr. Gustav Hilger, Hitler's deputy foreign minister. At one point, Hilger was actually being paid by the State Department and the CIA to serve as a consultant on the Soviet Union. Although Hilger is not specifically mentioned by name, a 1978 report published by the Government Accounting Office (GOA) makes mention of a senior member of the German Foreign Ministry who was reportedly brought to the United States by "the CIA [Central Intelligence Agency] director" due to his extensive knowledge of the Soviet Union.[11]

Until his death several years ago, Dr. Hilger maintained two residences—one in the United States, the other in West Germany. Hilger's wartime activities had included acting as a liaison between Hitler's minister of foreign affairs Joachim von Ribbentrop, who was hanged after being tried at Nuremberg, and an SS unit that had been responsible for the murder of approximately 1.4 million Soviet Jews on the Eastern Front.

In recent years, many people have taken the position that the U.S. government's early ties to former Nazis may be at least partially responsible for its delay in ferreting out and prosecuting war criminals. According to an article by William Bole, a 1985 investigation by the GAO

> found that United States agencies did bring known war criminals to America. Five out of twelve former Nazi cases reviewed by the congressional watchdog agency

had received help in immigration. This study followed a 1978 GAO investigation that discovered that the Federal Bureau of Investigation, the Central Intelligence Agency, the State Department, and the Defense Department all admitted to being in contact with alleged war criminals.[12]

In 1979, the Office of Special Investigations (OSI) was established as the U.S. Department of Justice's Nazi-hunting unit. In October 1984, the OSI made a public statement pertaining to Dr. Arthur Rudolph, one of the Mittelwerk scientists who had emigrated to the United States during Project Paperclip. Rudolph, who had been instrumental in designing the Saturn V rockets that launched American astronauts to the moon, had agreed to leave the United States and never return. Rudolph had been given the option of either permanently leaving the country or facing charges as a war criminal.

The investigation into his past revealed that Rudolph had allowed and at times encouraged worker beatings, torture, and even executions. For two years, Rudolph had been the chief operations director at the factory. In addition to his engineering duties, he authorized the slave laborers' living and working conditions. According to the Nazis' foreign laborers' program, foreign workers were to "be treated in such a way as to exploit them to the highest possible extent at the lowest conceivable degree of expenditure."[13]

Rudolph faithfully adhered to these guidelines. Even in freezing weather, he issued only pants and shirts of the thinnest material for his workers. They were fed only two bowls of broth a day, thereby receiving only half the nutrition needed to sustain life. Workers were not provided with drinking water, and there was no ventilation in the tunnels. Work shifts were twelve hours a day, seven days a week. The workers slept on the damp ground.

Sick workers were denied medical attention, and Rudolph refused to reduce their work schedules. Rudolph's laborers had a fifty-percent death rate. A significant number of Rudolph's workers were prisoners of war, although such treatment of captured military personnel violated the Hague and Geneva Conventions. At least one of the men was a member of the U.S. Air Force.[14]

As expressed in the *Bulletin of Atomic Scientists* at the time of the OSI announcement about Rudolph, it was assumed that Rudolph had accidentally slipped past "the watchful eyes of the officials who ran the Pentagon's Project Paperclip."[15] However, a startling April 1985 report in the *Bulletin of Atomic Scientists* revealed existing government documents indicating that U.S. military officials had actually known about Rudolph's World War II activities as well as the dubious backgrounds of a number of other Project Paperclip scientists. It was now public knowledge that the scientists' files had been whitewashed in order to allow them entry into the United States.

Perhaps the most notorious as well as the highest-ranking Nazi collaborator ever to come to the United States was a man by the name of Andrija Artukovic. Even after the first charges against him as a war criminal surfaced in the early 1950s, the FBI continued to use him as an informant. Artukovic, known as the Butcher of the Balkans, had served as interior minister in the Nazi state of Croatia during World

War II. While active within the Nazi regime, Artukovic was held responsible for the brutal murder of approximately seven hundred thousand Serbs, Jews, Gypsies, and others.

In an early attempt to escape justice following the war, Artukovic had traveled through Italy, Switzerland, and Ireland. Using false papers, he finally managed to emigrate to the United States in 1948. Artukovic settled in California, where he worked as a bookkeeper. But before long, his whereabouts became known to his pursuers. As early as 1951, Andrija Artukovic had begun fighting off extradition measures for his return to Yugoslavia to stand trial.

Finally in 1984, at eighty-six years of age, Artukovic was sent back to Yugoslavia to be tried for his crimes. Supreme Court Justice William Rehnquist denied the old and feeble Nazi's request for a stay. U.S. marshals later escorted Andrija Artukovic aboard a JAT airlines flight to Yugoslavia.

At first, Artukovic seemed oblivious to what was happening to him. Then, as the airplane's seat belt sign flashed in Serbo-Croatian, the returning prisoner spoke for the first time. He simply said, "Now I know where I'm going."[16] After nearly half a century of delays, Andrija Artukovic would finally have to answer for his crimes.

Nazi-war-criminal-researcher Charles Allen, Jr., also discovered the actual identities of thirty-seven alleged Nazi war criminals who were being investigated by OSI. All but three had been used by the government in one way or another.[17] As a result of the investigations of their past activities, several individuals had been deported. In some instances, however, their deportation has proven not to be a very severe punishment. For example, Romanian Orthodox archbishop Valerian Trifa was accused of inciting riots against the Jews in 1941. The angry mobs subsequently hung the Jews on meat racks and then slit their throats in the same manner in which kosher cattle are butchered. The archbishop was deported to a sunny and beautiful beach area of Portugal in 1984. His social security benefit payments are sent to him there.

Generally, deportees are no longer entitled to such benefits. However, the only exception applies to individuals deported for "activities conducted under the direction of, or in association with, the Nazi government during World War II."[18] This specification was originally designed as an inducement to encourage scientists involved in Project Paperclip to emigrate to the United States. However, Charles E. Schumer, Democratic congressman from Brooklyn, New York, has introduced legislation to revoke this exemption.

John Loftus, a private attorney in Rockland, Massachusetts, was formerly an investigator with the OSI. Through a thorough investigation of possible Nazi war criminals, Mr. Loftus found that United States intelligence agencies had actively recruited and paved the way for a number of leaders of the Byelorussian Nazi occupation government. Among these was Stanislaw Stankievich, a Queens, New York, resident who had found a job with Radio Free Europe. During the war, Stankievich had often been referred to as the "Butcher of Borissow." Among his other unsavory activities, Stanislaw Stankievich had also run a newspaper that preached the systematic annihilation of all Jewish people as well as the crushing defeat of the Allied powers by Nazi Germany.

Stankievich had been cited in the April 1985 GAO list of alleged war criminals who were brought into the United States with government help. During the late 1970s, the OSI had taken steps to revoke Stankievich's citizenship. However, he died during the investigation.

A similar case involved a man named Anton Adamovitch who, in May 1982, was interviewed on the CBS television documentary program "60 Minutes." In the taped interview, Mr. Adamovitch openly admitted having been a Nazi propagandist and collaborator during the Byelorussian regime. He also stated that he had acted as an informer for the United States government. Adamovitch claimed that in return for his assistance, the FBI had granted him entrance to this country despite its knowledge of his past.

At times, Nazi war criminals have received assistance from some unlikely sources. Newly declassified U.S. documents indicate that American officials in Rome did not apprehend Ante Pavelic, a wanted war criminal and leader of the Nazi puppet state of Croatia, because of his high-level contacts with the Vatican. The documents state that church officials hid Pavelic, and assisted him in his escape to Argentina. They also indicate that Vatican officials were fully aware of the situation.

Pavelic neared the head of the list of war criminals that the Allies had formally agreed to return to Yugoslavia for trial. He is accused of having overseen hundreds of thousands of deaths during the Nazi takeover.

The allegation involving the Roman Catholic church and the U.S. government was derived from high-level U.S. intelligence reports retrieved from the National Archives in Washington, D.C., and Fort Meade, Maryland, where the intelligence files had been stored. The documents had previously been classified by the U.S. government in order to protect Allied governments and the Vatican from potential embarrassment. Then, in 1985, when the documents were finally declassified, they were obtained by former OSI investigator John Loftus, who released them to the Religious News Service.

As one memorandum dated September 12, 1947, and signed by three agents of the U.S. Army's Counter-Intelligence Corps detachment in Rome stated: "Pavelic's contacts are so high and his present position is so compromising to the Vatican that any extradition of subject [Pavelic] would deal a staggering blow to the Roman Catholic church."[19]

The authenticity of this report and similar ones that originated from the Army unit in Rome was confirmed by the Freedom of Information Office of the U.S. Intelligence Security Command at Fort Meade. According to the *National Catholic Reporter*, "The documents shed new light on allegations that have surfaced in the past that the Catholic church helped accused war criminals escape from Europe. While previous revelations have centered primarily on the activities of priests in Rome, the new documents detail the U.S. government's assessment of the Vatican's role in the operations."[20]

Open allegations that the U.S. government itself had actually been involved in aiding and abetting Nazi war criminals have only recently penetrated the public's awareness. According to former U.S. representative Elizabeth Holtzman, who has sponsored legislation barring Nazi war criminals from the United States, "We now know more than we did in 1974. I had no idea at that time that the U.S. government was involved in bringing these people here. The CIA lied to me when I chaired the subcommittee on immigration and it denied this."[21]

Ms. Holtzman feels that the various reports that point to alleged relationships between the U.S. government and Nazi collaborators underscore the need for an open inquiry to examine the matter. She said: "This is needed to prevent any repetition in the future. The U.S. should not become a haven for other war criminals or torturers who work for U.S. intelligence agencies in the same way it did for former Nazi war criminals."[22]

Exposing and deporting Nazi war criminals is not often pursued without considerable embarrassment to U.S. government officials. Often, agencies and officials try to defend the assistance given to former Nazi party members and collaborators as a necessary response to the cold war and the dearth of anticommunist intelligence data available at the time. Deporting those who committed genocide was regarded as less important than warding off the possible threat of Russian dominance.

Still another reason why so many Nazi war criminals may have emigrated to the U.S. may have less to do with governmental need than with widespread anti-Jewish sentiments throughout the country. It may be argued that an examination of the Displaced Persons Act of 1948 reveals that the act may have actually been tailored to exclude large numbers of concentration camp victims while allowing other ethnic Germans to gain entrance.[23]

Nevertheless, since the Justice Department established the Office of Special Investigations in 1979, numerous naturalized Americans have been stripped of their citizenship because of their Nazi pasts. In addition to those individuals who have already been deported, over six hundred additional cases are presently under investigation.[24]

※ As a result, at times Nazi war criminals have been brought to trial even when they might have thought they had found a safe haven in America. One such case is that of John (Ivan) Demjanjuk, a sadistic guard at the Treblinka death camp who operated the camp's gas chambers as well as tortured countless persons with whips, iron rods, and bayonets. He was known to have performed his work with gusto and insatiable cruelty. Witnesses have stated that he had split open heads, cut off ears, gouged out eyes, and ripped open the bellies of pregnant women. In fact, Demjanjuk's inhumane deeds had earned him the title of "Ivan the Terrible" among the prison inmates.

Within a one-year period ending in the summer of 1943, the Nazis murdered eight hundred and seventy thousand Polish Jews in Treblinka's gas chambers. It took approximately a half-hour for the carbon monoxide to asphyxiate the victims locked within these death enclosures.

At Treblinka, John Demjanjuk operated a truck engine that released the carbon monoxide into the chamber confines. Treblinka survivors have testified that at times Demjanjuk didn't even turn on the gas. Instead, he left those inside to slowly suffocate.

John (Ivan) Demjanjuk gained entrance into the United States by falsifying information on his immigration papers. He settled in Parma, Ohio, and became a U.S. citizen. Demjanjuk raised a family and was employed as an auto-engine mechanic at the Ford plant in Cleveland. He went to St. Vladimir's Ukrainian church and tended his lush vegetable garden. Demjanjuk said he'd been a farmer during World War II.

In 1981, after the Soviets produced an old identification card in response to a Justice Department query about Demjanjuk's war record, the United States revoked Demjanjuk's U.S. citizenship. In 1986, the United States allowed him to be extradited to Israel to stand trial for his crimes.

Ivan the Terrible's trial once again focused the world's attention on the Holocaust. The trial was broadcast live from the actual courtroom, as Israel was eager to have its young people learn what it was like for Jews under the Nazis during World War II. Young Israelis stood in line to be afforded an opportunity to witness this long-awaited date with justice. As one twenty-one-year-old student from Hebrew University said of Demjanjuk's trial, "It's a privilege to witness the judgment of crimes that for my generation seem like long-gone history."[25]

At one point, even the Polish-born Israeli prime minister, Yitzhak Shamir, visited the trial scene. His entire family had been killed during the Holocaust. People throughout the country followed the trial attentively through radio broadcasts.

During Demjanjuk's trial, camp survivors related hideous tales of torture and mass murder at Treblinka. The last time such horrors had been detailed in an Israeli courtroom was over a quarter of a century ago in the trial of Nazi war criminal Adolf Eichmann. It was essential to the Israelis that Demjanjuk also come face-to-face with justice. As poet Haim Gouri, who as a young journalist covered the Eichmann trial, said of the proceedings, "The charges against Demjanjuk are so devastating that a nation which would not put him on trial would be denying its own self-respect, culture and history."[26]

Both prior to and during the proceedings, Demjanjuk claimed that he was not Ivan the Terrible, and that the charges against him amounted to nothing more than a case of mistaken identity. The accused insisted that an important piece of evidence against him, an SS identification card provided by the Soviet Union, was actually a forgery. At one point during the trial, Demjanjuk even turned to the crowds and cameras and shouted, "Mistake!"[27]

From the first day of the trial, the bald, thick-necked Demjanjuk smiled and acted in a receptive, friendly manner to those present in the courtroom. Often, he called out pleasant greetings in Hebrew to those surrounding him. His opportunistic overtures were not generally well received.

When he attempted to shake hands with sixty-five-year-old Treblinka survivor Eliahu Rosenberg, the man turned to Demjanjuk and screamed, "It is Ivan from Treblinka, from the gas chambers—the man I am looking at this very moment. I saw the eyes, the murderous eyes, and the face. And how dare you give me a hand, you murderer."[28] As Rosenberg recoiled from Demjanjuk's hand, the Treblinka survivor's wife fainted in the courtroom.

Other witnesses identified John Demjanjuk as Ivan the Terrible as well. Seventy-two-year-old Yehiel Reichman, who had remained at Treblinka for

Facing Page: John Demjanjuk (left) steps onto Israeli soil in handcuffs following his extradition from the United States. He is accompanied by a translator and Israeli police personnel. Above: This is a blown-up photograph of Demjanjuk from a pass issued to him by the German SS in 1942. Demjanjuk claimed that the pass had been falsified and that he is not Ivan the Terrible.

eleven months prior to his escape during a prisoners' revolt, became the fifth witness to positively identify Demjanjuk. Reichman told the court, "This devil I carried within me. I saw him every step I took every night, every day. I saw him in everything I did."[29]

The white-haired witness stunned trial spectators as he described the hideous conditions at Treblinka and Ivan the Terrible's role in the horrors. He said:

> A poor trembling woman was holding a baby in the corner of the barracks. A German took the baby from this woman and smashed the head of the baby against the wall, and of course, it was killed. . . . He [Ivan the Terrible] was the worst devil of all at Treblinka. And I often shudder at the thought of what a two-legged animal he was, capable of perpetrating such deeds.[30]

Another Treblinka survivor, sixty-two-year-old Pinchas Epstein, had been forced to carry the corpses to the pit, which he claims afforded him "an excellent view of Ivan." Epstein said: "I saw him all the time. We were in a small area. . . . He looked with pleasure at mutilated corpses only meters away from me. I can't find words to find any compassion for him, he was not of this planet. . . . He was a monster out of this world."[31]

Epstein went on to describe Demjanjuk's deeds: "Ivan would push people into the gas chambers, beating them with a pipe and slashing them with a bayonet or sword. On one occasion," said Epstein, on the verge of tears,

> a twelve-year-old girl was taken alive from the gas chamber. She was moaning for her mother. Ivan the Terrible ordered a young prisoner to drop his pants and have sex with the child. The prisoner just lay on top of

the girl and did nothing. She was later taken to a pit and shot. He did this to shame the girl. I can't even compare him to an animal. If a wild beast has sated its appetite, it stops; but Ivan was never sated.[32]

The three-judge tribunal in the Jerusalem courtroom found the retired Cleveland auto worker guilty. He was convicted of crimes against humanity. The court stated: "The accused wasn't an ordinary guard who just obeyed orders. . . . With his own hands, he took part in the murders of masses of human beings."[33]

Another Nazi war criminal recently deported from the United States is Karl Linnas. During the early 1940s, Linnas was chief of a Nazi concentration camp in his native country of Estonia (now part of the Soviet Union). Over twelve thousand Eastern Europeans lost their lives there. Approximately two thousand of the victims were Jews.

Under Linnas's authority, half-clothed men, women, and children were made to stand in front of mass graves, where they were shot. Some were actually gunned down by Linnas himself. After giving the order to fire, it was not uncommon for Linnas to pull out his pistol and finish off any survivors.

The charges against Linnas were supported both by the testimony of survivors and Nazi records and documents recovered from the camp. In 1962 a court in the Soviet Union tried Karl Linnas in absentia for war crimes, found him guilty, and sentenced him to death.

For a time, Linnas remained unaffected by the Soviet tribunal's verdict. When found guilty, he was residing in Greenlawn, New York. He had become a U.S. citizen in 1960, nine years after coming to this country.

Karl Linnas's case lay dormant until the Justice Department established the Office of Special Investigations (OSI) in 1979. Then, OSI attorneys obtained the Kremlin's permission to visit Estonia and question Soviet eyewitnesses about Linnas's activities during World War II.

The lawyers returned with documents and videotaped depositions confirming Karl Linnas's guilt. They then persuaded a U.S. district court to begin proceedings to strip Linnas of his U.S. citizenship on the grounds that the former Nazi had lied about his World War II activities to U.S. immigration officials. In 1981, Linnas's citizenship was formally revoked, as the court found the case against Linnas to be "uncontrovertible."[34] Karl Linnas unsuccessfully appealed the decision all the way up to the Supreme Court.

Shortly thereafter, the Justice Department initiated deportation proceedings. Linnas pursued whatever measures were available to fend off deportation. There were over a dozen trials, hearings, and reviews. When it became obvious that he'd be sent back to the Soviet Union, Linnas tried to seek asylum elsewhere. However, after two dozen other countries turned him down, in 1987 Karl Linnas found himself under Soviet guard being escorted onto a special Soviet plane. Hours later, he arrived to meet his fate in a country in which he'd been tried and sentenced to death over twenty-five years earlier.

Other war criminals have recently been deported as well. In May 1990, accused Nazi mass murderer Josef Schwammberger was deported from Argentina to stand trial in West Germany for killing about 5,000 Jews. Schwammberger had initially been arrested in

Karl Linnas, who had been sentenced to death by the Soviets, arrives in Tallinn, the capital of Estonia, a Soviet republic on the Baltic Sea. Linnas was deported from the United States after being tried by the Soviets in absentia on charges that he ran a Nazi concentration camp in Tartu, Estonia, during World War II.

1947 by French authorities, but he escaped and fled to Argentina. There he pursued a quiet existence for nearly forty years until his arrest in 1987 by Argentine police.

Schwammberger has been described by the Simon Wiesenthal Center for Holocaust Studies as one of the world's most-sought-after criminals. Survivors of concentration camps in Poland have accused him of smashing children's heads against walls and personally throwing men, women, and children into bonfires. Rabbi Marvin Hier of the Simon Wiesenthal Center said of Schwammberger's trial: "This will be a historic case because it will be the first trial of a war criminal since the fall of the Berlin Wall. Millions of East Germans, who have never heard of Nazi atrocities, will now hear firsthand accounts."[35]

Still another case involves a man named Bohdan Kozly, who fled from the United States to a villa in a lush green valley of Costa Rica. While tending the rows of coffee bushes and fruit trees that flourish on his seven-acre estate, Kozly regrets an error of his past. As he said, "I made a mistake." With tears flooding his eyes, he added, "I came to the United States."[36]

Kozly was forced to leave his home in Fort Lauderdale, Florida, after being ferreted out by the OSI as a Nazi war criminal. The United States charged Kozly with being a Nazi collaborator involved in the murder of Jews. However, on the United States citizenship application he had filled out in 1956, Kozly had taken care to conceal his former affiliations. The only group to which he admitted being a member had been the "Boy Scouts."

During Kozly's deportation trial, a number of witnesses described his murderous acts during the

Nazi occupation of their Ukrainian town. They testified that Kozly executed as many as fourteen Jews, four of whom were children. A Jewish woman had been caring for one small girl after the child's parents, her friends, had been seized by the Nazis. When the woman and child were later captured, they fell into Kozly's hands. "He [Kozly] took the child out of my arms," the woman said. "The child started screaming, 'Mommy, Mommy!' I was crying. He pushed me through the door. I never saw the child again."[37] Another witness testified that he watched Kozly drag the little girl from the building. The witness added, "Then he stepped back—let's say it was around ten steps from her—and he shot the child."[38]

Anton Vatseb, now in his sixties, was a teenager at the time he watched Kozly's killing spree. According to Vatseb, "He had a great passion, a passion for killing people."[39]

The trial ended with an order to deport Kozly to Russia. Kozly fought the decision for three years, but the deportation order was upheld. At that point, Kozly sold his Florida motel and left the country with his wife. They fled to Costa Rica, where they secured resident visas.

However, Bohdan Kozly's good fortune did not prevail. Costa Rica later ruled in favor of a Soviet request for his extradition to stand trial in the USSR for war crimes.

Although Bohdan Kozly had never met Max Kandler, a New York wallet manufacturer, their lives are irrevocably intertwined. In 1948 Max Kandler and his wife had emigrated to the United States, where they raised their three sons. The couple rarely spoke about the war. Max Kandler's entire family had been killed in the Holocaust.

Kandler thought the ordeal was over, but that

wasn't the case. At Bohdan Kozly's trial, Max Kandler learned how his relatives had perished. Seven members of Max Kandler's family were marched into the town's graveyard for Jews, where they were shot by Kozly and a German.

According to a witness, "One of the women pleaded with Kozly to let her live, but he pushed her away and continued firing."[40] Other witnesses claimed that the following day Kozly returned to have his photograph taken among the nude, still unburied corpses.

Among the recent targets of Nazi hunters has been Alois Brunner. Brunner, who was one of Adolf Eichmann's chief assistants, is personally responsible for sending over 140,000 Jews to their deaths. Although the Syrian government has denied any knowledge of his existence, he is known to be protected by armed guard while residing in his Damascus apartment. Efforts continue to apprehend this key figure of the Nazi regime.

At times, conservative spokespersons have argued that present-day trials of alleged Nazi war criminals might be tainted. They stress that legal proceedings based on incidents that took place forty years earlier cannot be fair. However, in response, the prosecuting attorneys have stressed that often there is such a preponderance of evidence that these men would have been convicted at any time under any circumstances. For individuals who lost their families and had their own lives shattered through Nazi atrocities, there can never be a statute of limitations on war crimes.

4

KLAUS BARBIE — THE BUTCHER OF LYONS

Nazi war criminal Klaus Barbie was born on October 25, 1913, in a small, quiet town near the Rhine River. His parents, who did not marry until three months after their son's birth, named him Nikolaus ("Klaus"). Only a marginal student, Barbie finally managed to pass his graduation exams in 1934 after several unsuccessful tries.

At that time, Hitler had already been Germany's chancellor for about a year, and Barbie found himself drawn to the ideology espoused by the nation's new leader. As Barbie wrote, "This year's events have left me restless. Like every other true German, I am attracted by the powerful national movement, and today I serve alongside all others who follow the Führer.[1]"

Barbie joined the Hitler Youth Movement and also became the personal assistant of the local Nazi party leader. As Tom Bowker cites in his book, *Klaus Barbie, the Butcher of Lyons*: "He [Barbie] relished the life-style, comradeship, and self-importance that attachment to the Party gave. As he admitted forty years later in Bolivia, he became a life-long Nazi dedicated to Hitler and German supremacy and learnt a violent contempt for those who failed the racial and moral tests which the SS state immortalized."[2]

Barbie joined the SS and within a short period of time had begun taking an active role in carrying out its brutal policies. Early on in his Nazi career, Barbie was sent to Holland during the German occupation. As the Germans began to implement their racist policies, the pressure on the Jewish population mounted.

Then on May 14, 1941, a bomb exploded in a German officers' club in the Jewish sector of Amsterdam. Although it was rumored that the bombing had been the work of a local Resistance group, the Germans were determined that the Jews would pay for the incident.

To implement their strategy for revenge, Barbie paid a call on the two co-presidents of the Jewish Council. The Council was an organization established by the Germans to represent Dutch Jews. When Barbie arrived at their office on the morning of June 11, the co-presidents, Abraham Asscher and David Cohen, were amazed at his gentle manner and cordial demeanor. Barbie told the men that he had come to rectify a situation that would benefit Holland's Jews.

At one point, the Germans had decided that three hundred Jewish apprentices would have to abandon

The only known photograph of Klaus Barbie as an SS officer in Nazi uniform

their desirable training positions. Barbie said they had reconsidered and now wished to return the young men to their former posts. He said that he needed a list of the boys' names and addresses in order to write to them to inform them of this generous change in policy. Cohen readily supplied Barbie with the necessary list, and Barbie left the premises as politely as he had arrived.

That afternoon, both Cohen and Asscher were summoned to police headquarters. At first, this didn't seem like an unusual request. However, once the men arrived, they were detained there the entire afternoon without being offered any explanation as to why they'd been sent for.

Finally, by early evening, Asscher was given permission to call home. He listened in horror as he was told of the events that had taken place within the Jewish community during that afternoon. A massive roundup of young Jewish apprentices had been accomplished by the Germans. Cohen and Asscher had been corralled at the station to prevent them from warning the boys once they realized what was happening.

Later that evening, the co-presidents pleaded with the SS commander in charge to be merciful, but their requests were ignored. The SS commander said the boys had been arrested in retaliation for the May 14 bombing of the German officers' club. The young Dutch apprentices were deported to a concentration camp and were all dead within a year. Some had been used in the early gassing experiments which had begun that summer.

The callousness Barbie exhibited in Holland was just a prelude to an extensive and sadistic career within the Third Reich. Perhaps the most infamous era of Barbie's crimes against humanity occurred during the period he served as Germany's wartime head of the Gestapo in France's third-largest city, Lyons. The following are among the deeds that earned him the title of "The Butcher of Lyons":

- In February 1943, Barbie ordered eighty-six Jews at Lyons's Union Générale des Israélites de France to be rounded up. Out of this number, he had seventy-six sent to death camps. Only five survived the experience.
- In August 1944, Barbie deported three hundred Jews along with another three hundred French Resistance prisoners. They were sent to the death camps of Auschwitz and Buchenwald for immediate extermination. He completed this action although he knew that the advancing Allied armies would liberate the city of Lyons within a matter of days.
- A continuous series of arrests, deportations, and executions of members of the French Resistance movement. Among these was the torture-murder of the legendary hero Jean Moulin. Moulin, Charles de Gaulle's deputy who headed the French Resistance, had been personally tortured by Barbie in 1943.
- In addition to these murders, thousands of Jews in Lyons were savagely dragged from their homes for deportation. Often the weakest of these were singled out for some special brutality or received an immediate bullet in the head.

Among Barbie's most horrendous acts was the one that involved forty-one children, ranging in age from three to thirteen, from The Jewish Children's Home in Izieu, France, about forty miles from Lyons. On Barbie's orders, the Gestapo raided the school and grabbed the children while they were having breakfast.

The little ones were then pitched, as though they were parcels, into the backs of two trucks that waited outside the building. Screaming as they were torn from their protectors, these children were sent to Auschwitz to be exterminated. A single teacher from this children's school was the sole survivor of the experience.

Another survivor of Barbie's brutal regime was Lise Lesèvre, a French housewife who, in 1944, was interrogated for nineteen hours regarding her activities in France's anti-Nazi Resistance movement. Attempting to induce the woman to furnish him with the names of others active in the Resistance, Barbie mercilessly tortured Lesèvre during her captivity. She was stripped of her clothing and beaten into unconsciousness. According to *Newsweek*: "She was submerged in frozen bath water until her lungs nearly burst. Handcuffs with spikes on the inside were tightened around her wrists until the metal ate into her flesh. 'Who is Didier? Where is Didier?' Barbie repeatedly demanded, referring to the code name of a Resistance leader."[3]

Lise Lesèvre was only a minor figure in the Resistance; she had no knowledge of the information Barbie sought. Nevertheless, even after he realized that Lesèvre couldn't help him, he continued his barbarous mistreatment of her. Barbie enjoyed inflicting torture on others under the guise of interrogation.

As Mme. Lesèvre described his actions: "The remarkable thing about Barbie was the absolute joy he took in making others suffer. . . . Several times I saw Barbie raise, with the point of his boot, the head of a prisoner sprawled on the floor, barely still alive after torture. When he believed he recognized a Jew, Barbie would give the prisoner a kick in the face."[4]

Barbie was often bizarre in his systematic cruelty to his victims. He would inject someone with poison or leave "victims dangling from hooks while a smiling Barbie occasionally paused to play a love song on a nearby piano."[5]

Claiming that her charges against Barbie were not solely based on memory, Lise Lesèvre produced a small diary that she kept in 1944. She had personally retained a carefully documented record of everything that happened to her in prison as well as in the cells where Barbie tortured his victims. At first, she would scribble notes on scraps of paper, which she carefully hid in the soles of her shoes. Later, after being sent to a concentration camp, she recorded the hideous events in a small notebook she miraculously managed to retain. It is a diary of her own hardship and pain as well as that of others.

Raymond Aubrac, another leader of the French Resistance, described Barbie as follows:

> Looking back, I sometimes even think that he wasn't interested in getting any information. Fundamentally, he was a sadist who enjoyed causing pain and proving his power. He had an extraordinary fund of violence. Coshes, clubs, and whips lay on his desk and he used them a lot. Contrary to what some others say, he wasn't even a good policeman, because he never got any information out of me. Not even my identity or that I was Jewish.[6]

Following Germany's fall, Barbie's name appeared on two lists of wanted war criminals. These lists stated that Barbie had been a Gestapo officer and was wanted for torture and murder. One list was published in London by the United Nations War Crimes Commission, and another published in Paris by CROWCASS, the Central Registry of War Crimes and Security Suspects.

Immediately following the war, it wasn't uncommon for the authorities to fail to identify and arrest the individuals who appeared on such lists. During this period, there was a great deal of disruption and disorganization at the lower levels of control, and in actuality, little had been done to create the necessary machinery to bring men such as Barbie to justice.

However, as Barbie hid out in Germany after the war, he still feared being apprehended. As it turned out, after a few years, it seemed as if his fears had been unfounded. For the time being, Barbie would not only escape French justice, he would even be recruited by U.S. Army Counterintelligence as an anticommunist agent in the spring of 1947.

Barbie's good fortune was an ironic circumstance of the times. A year earlier, he probably would have been prosecuted for the atrocities he committed as an SS Gestapo head. However, European politics had shifted and divisions between countries were beginning to solidify. The cold war had begun, and America's negative feelings toward the communists had heightened. Relationships between both nations and individuals were adjusted accordingly—now former friends were regarded with suspicion, and at times hunted war criminals were reevaluated in terms of their possible usefulness.

American intelligence agencies were eager to learn the Soviets' true intentions, as they were determined not to allow communism to spread to West

Germany. Today, the American official who initially recruited Barbie claims that he doesn't even remember meeting him. He's stated that at the time Barbie simply appeared to be another German with a "dirty past."[7]

Following the end of the war, many of the more talented American intelligence officers were eager to return home. As the top men sought assignments in the United States, unfortunately those left behind often didn't have a clear understanding of the situation in Germany and lacked fluency in the language. Many were unsuited for the work assigned to them, and eventually these men proved to be less willing to remove incriminated Nazis from positions of power.[8]

At the time Barbie came to work for the United States, the mood had changed appreciably from that of the immediate postwar period. Much of the initial zeal in the denazification process and the punishment of Nazi war criminals had evaporated. The Russians had become the primary target of America's concerns.

It was under these circumstances that Klaus Barbie—the Butcher of Lyons—began his assignments for America's intelligence service. The only condition of his employment was that he agree to discontinue contact "with other SS or German intelligence personnel" unless he was so instructed by his superiors. Without seeming to think twice about it, Barbie readily agreed to these terms.

Barbie proved successful in his espionage assignments. His supervisor wrote about him: "Since Barbie started to work for this agent, he has provided extensive connections to high-ranking Romanian circles and to high Russian aides in the U.S. zone. . . .

It is felt that his value as an informant infinitely out-weighs any use he may have in prison."[9]

Despite the fact that by the beginning of 1948 it wasn't uncommon to use incriminated Germans as the need arose, Barbie's freedom in Europe was soon to be seriously threatened. By May of 1948, the French had become aware that the Americans were using Barbie and had begun to press for his extradition to France. As was reported in the book *Klaus Barbie, The Butcher of Lyons*, "On May 14th, a Paris newspaper briefly reported protests to the American ambassador by Lyons Resistance groups about the employment of Barbie. The piece summarized Barbie's terror tactics in the region, including the use of an acetylene torch in interrogations."[10]

Up until that period, the Americans had tried to justify their use of Barbie on the grounds that they hadn't been aware of the extent of his war crimes, despite an abundance of available evidence to document his multiple atrocities. Their primary interest in Barbie was in his usefulness as an effective tool in the fight against communism. Nevertheless, as time passed, it became too embarrassing for the Americans to continue using Barbie. Pressure from the French for his extradition to stand trial persisted, and Barbie was now turning into a liability.

One agent later reported that shortly thereafter it came to his attention that Barbie's entire family had been learning Spanish. They were simply preparing an escape to South America. At that point, even Barbie was anxious for a departure date, as he feared he might be kidnapped by French agents at any time.

Barbie's escape to South America was prearranged by American intelligence agents. He and his family left Europe by means of the "Ratline," a well-funded route established by the American intelligence service. The Ratline had been designed to transport American agents, as well as other important contacts who had become vulnerable, to safe areas.

An agent who had been instrumental in setting up the Ratline described how the service worked: "As a reward for services, we settled them in different parts of the world." He went on to detail the methodical and well-rehearsed nature of Ratline expeditions:

> We never let a Ratline product out of sight. The escort (often a three-man team) would baby-sit in the hotel, not letting the shipment out of sight until the ship's departure. Then we would walk him right up to the gangplank, turn him over to somebody aboard ship who knew this was a special person who had to be taken care of, and that was the end of the Ratline.[11]

Individuals who took the Ratline route to safety might be furnished with anywhere from one thousand to eight thousand dollars with which to start over in a new country. Although different sums have been quoted, it is rumored that Klaus Barbie received five thousand dollars.

Leo Hecht, a twenty-three-year-old German Jew, was the intelligence service's contact in helping Barbie evade justice via the Ratline. Hecht had been ordered to prepare the Barbie family for evacuation. He acquired passports for them, suitcases, and other incidentals they'd need on the trip. Hecht even arranged for a farewell visit between Barbie and his mother. It is ironic that a Jewish contact had been

A photograph of Barbie's passport. The passport, which was secured with American help, permitted the ex-Nazi to escape from Germany with his family.

so instrumental in assisting Barbie to escape. If the two had met during the war, less than a decade earlier, Barbie most likely would have had Hecht deported to a death camp. Now it was Hecht's responsibility to see that Barbie safely arrived at his new destination.

Barbie and his family settled in Bolivia. Taking the name Klaus Altmann, Barbie now enjoyed a peaceful life as a prosperous businessman. He made a good deal of money illegally as an arms runner. He also secretly became useful to the Bolivian government, as he relied on his past experiences to offer a string of South American dictators advice on handling what they perceived as security problems.

Twice while Barbie remained in hiding, France tried him in absentia. In both 1952 and 1954, Klaus Barbie was found guilty and sentenced to death for complicity in the murder of nearly twelve thousand people.

As it turned out, it was a dedicated husband-and-wife team of Nazi hunters, Serge and Beate Klarsfeld, who relentlessly tracked down the brutal Butcher of Lyons. Serge, a French-Jewish attorney from Paris whose father had died in Auschwitz, and his German-born wife Beate were determined to bring the mass murderer back to Europe to face his victims. The couple worked diligently with Itta Halaunbrenner, a woman who had lost two children at the Izieu school. When they finally ascertained Barbie's whereabouts, in 1971, the couple launched a worldwide campaign to have him arrested.

For eleven years, the Klarsfelds ardently fought for Barbie's return, but the various Bolivian dictators in power were not about to succumb to their pressure tactics. The Klarsfelds refused to abandon their goal. In 1972, Beate Klarsfeld appeared in chains in the Bolivian capital to draw attention to Barbie's presence in the country and to dramatize Bolivia's link to Nazism. She also placed an advertisement in a newspaper, as a personal challenge to Barbie, which read, "Come to France and stand trial."[12] Barbie never replied.

Instead, he used his safe haven to brag about his past affiliations. As Tom Bowker says in his book, "Ever since he had been discovered hiding in Bolivia in 1971, Klaus Barbie had boasted provocatively about his love for Adolf Hitler, his undying devotion to Nazism, and how he humiliated the French Resistance in Lyons. His scornful defiance of the French had wounded his surviving victims, and the Klarsfelds were determined on revenge."[13] In fact, at one point the Paris-based couple even admitted that if they weren't able to bring Barbie back to France to stand trial, they had considered having him killed in South America. As Beate Klarsfeld reported:

> Barbie would have been killed. Serge and I felt responsible for the mothers of the children he had murdered. It was inconceivable to us that the mothers would one day die, having suffered terrible anguish for forty years, and Barbie still would be enjoying his life. We always told the mothers that killing would be an act of despair, a defeat, but that we had to be prepared to kill him if we couldn't find a legal solution. It would still have been a success.[14]

In the early 1980s, circumstances began to change for Barbie. As *Time* described the turn of events, "Barbie's political connections [had] thwarted French efforts at extradition. Finally, during a brief period of civilian rule in 1983, the authorities in La Paz, Bolivia, handed him over to the French."[15]

By the time Barbie was returned to France, the country had already banned the death penalty. That meant that if convicted, life imprisonment was the severest sentence he could receive. There were legal problems involved in charging Barbie as well.

A twenty-year statute of limitations on war crimes in France made it impossible to retry him on old charges, such as the murder of [the French Resistance leader] Jean Moulin. Instead, he was accused of crimes against humanity. Among them: the arrest, deportation and murder of other Resistance fighters, and the deportation of the children of Izieu, and some four hundred other French Jews.[16]

Despite his apprehension and arrest, Barbie remained unrepentent for his past deeds. Ignoring the mountain of evidence against him, Barbie insisted that he was free of guilt. As he said in an interview smuggled out of the prison where he awaited trial: "I was hard but never cruel. . . . I am not an Eichmann."[17] Barbie accused his victims, insisting that any Nazi crimes committed in France wouldn't have been possible without the assistance of French collaborators. As was stated in *U.S. News & World Report*, "Klaus Barbie—the Butcher of Lyons—boasted that the French would never be able 'to hold their heads high' after he exposed their wartime collaboration."[18]

Unfortunately, the reality of France's cooperation with Nazi forces during the German occupation could have posed some embarrassment to the country as Barbie stood trial. As expressed in an editorial by Harold Evans in *U.S. News & World Report*,

"The Gestapo, with only 2,500 men in all France, could not have conducted its reign of terror without French bureaucrats, French police, pro-fascist volunteers, anti-Semites and others ready to denounce Jews in the hope of acquiring their apartments."[19]

Today, French historians and writers are beginning to acknowledge what is perhaps a more realistic version of France's role during the German occupation. There were numerous instances of overt anti-Semitism. *U.S. News & World Report* described the circumstances as follows:

> In fact, the ghosts that haunt Barbie also haunt France— and to some degree the United States as well. They are the long-repressed memories of a nation that has never quite come to grips with its wartime past. . . . Indeed, in the treatment of its own Jews, occupied France was at its ignoble worst. While some Christians hid Jews, a shocking number turned their backs.
>
> The Vichy regime [the government of occupied France] adopted anti-Semitic laws long before the Nazis asked it to. A village farmer betrayed the children of Izieu. Of the 76,000 Jews shipped to the death camps by France, 90 percent were arrested by enthusiastic French police and swaggering members of the fascist French militia.[20]

Although Barbie's date with justice was long overdue, there were those who feared that the trial might open old wounds which they'd hoped would have healed by now. Barbie's lawyer, Jacques Vergés, intensified their anxiety by promising to capitalize on France's role in the Nazi atrocities in order to defend his client. Vergés promised that part of his defense "will be to show the extensive local collaboration with Nazi occupiers, a chapter of the war that many Frenchmen would prefer to forget."[21]

Stressing that it was Barbie and not France who was being tried, there were many people who were anxious to see the court proceedings begin. Among them was Itta Halaunbrenner, whose two daughters were among the Izieu Jewish children whom Barbie had put to death. Mrs. Halaunbrenner, who had worked with the Klarsfelds for Barbie's arrest and extradition, had declared, "I will not sleep peacefully till Barbie has faced justice."[22]

Another woman, a former French Resistance worker, was also eager to testify against Barbie. She had been tortured by Barbie and sent to the Ravensbrück camp to die but had managed to survive. Her husband, along with one of her sons, had lost their lives in Nazi camps. Although the woman was aware that the trial would be an ordeal for France, she disagreed with those who said they would rather forget the period than have Barbie publicly tried. She stated: "To forget the crimes of the Nazis is unthinkable for us. We don't want vengeance; we want justice. We owe that to the memory of those who did not return."[23] Now in her late eighties, she claimed that the thought of one day testifying against Barbie had helped her to survive all these years.

This woman's sentiments were echoed by French historian Henri Amour, who told the French people, "Let us not make this hangman into the arbitrator of our quarrels or the judge of our history."[24]

Following his extradition, Barbie was held in Saint Joseph's prison in Lyons, France. Ironically, the prison is only a few hundred yards from Barbie's former Gestapo headquarters during World War II. He was kept in a solitary-confinement suite that afforded him the use of both a private shower and a well-stocked library.

Barbie kept somewhat of a routine schedule while awaiting trial. Each morning he rose at seven, spent thirty minutes exercising, watched television programs in the afternoon, and spent much of the remaining hours reading books. Although a talkative man by nature, the only people Barbie was permitted to speak to were his French guards, his defense attorney, and a daughter who visited him on a monthly basis.

Meanwhile, France began the preparations necessary to try an internationally infamous war criminal. It soon became apparent that there wasn't a courtroom in Lyons large enough to accommodate the crowds of people who would want to attend Barbie's trial. Instead, it was decided that Klaus Barbie would be tried in the immense entranceway of Lyons's Palace of Justice. According to *Newsweek*, "Lyons's grandiose Palace of Justice is being fitted with $200,000 worth of new lights, panels, and metal detectors for France's trial of the decade. Spectators will be able to buy tickets for more than 500 public seats, and for the first time in France the trial will be filmed—although the footage will not be shown for the next fifty years."[25]

The end result of the renovation was impressive. In addition to other seating, there were four hundred chairs for journalists from other countries. Along the walls in a makeshift balcony of sorts were approximately one hundred and fifty seats reserved for individuals who had claims against Barbie. Some of these people would be the grandchildren of victims who did not survive Barbie's torture sessions or his orders for their deportation to death camps.

Facing the victims and their survivors, three magistrates and nine jurors would be seated on a high dais. Approximately forty of the victims' attorneys were to be seated to the judges' right, while on the left, Barbie's attorney had a seat alone beneath the prisoner's dock.

In January 1987, Lise Lesèvre, one of the French Resistance workers whom Barbie had interrogated and tortured some forty years earlier, was brought to Lyons to confront Barbie personally during the pretrial investigation. When she saw Barbie in prison, she noted that he'd been well treated and wasn't even handcuffed during their interview. She felt it was quite a different setting from the blood-splattered cells in which Barbie had interrogated and tortured his prisoners during his days in the Gestapo.

Newsweek described the interaction between the two:

> Without looking at her, Barbie declared, "I don't know Mme. Lesèvre." She replied, "We were very close, you tortured me." Barbie insisted: "I never tortured women." From that point on, Lesèvre says, she was no longer afraid of Barbie, just angry. She found his denial an outrage and three times made him repeat that he never tortured women: "I wanted to say, 'All right, then how many men did you torture?' But I decided to save that for the trial."[26]

Stressing that she was not afraid of facing Barbie in public, Lesèvre added, "I will tell as much as I can at the trial. The world needs to know."[27]

The trial of Klaus Barbie lasted a full eight weeks. Throughout the proceedings, he showed no regrets for what he had done and demonstrated very little interest in defending himself. In fact, at the close of the trial, when he was asked if he had anything to say for himself, Barbie contended that he wasn't guilty of any general wrongdoing and stated, "That was the war and the war is over."[28]

For much of the proceedings, Barbie exercised his right under French law not to be present in the courtroom. As described by *Maclean's* magazine:

> The defendant [Barbie] stunned the court on May 13 by announcing that he was leaving the court. After patiently listening to a long series of statements followed by brief questions from the judges, Barbie declared himself to be "the victim of a kidnapping" [from Bolivia] and demanded his return to the Saint Joseph Prison in Lyons, where he had been since 1983 in a comfortable four-room suite.[29]

According to *Maclean's*, Barbie's attorney, Jacques Vergés, explained that Barbie "had adopted the tactic on the advice of a Bolivian lawyer who was contesting his expulsion from that country. But lawyer and Nazi hunter Serge Klarsfeld, who was representing many Jewish plaintiffs in the case, declared, 'Finally, the executioner showed he was weaker than his victims.'"[30]

Barbie appeared in court for the three initial days of the trial and later was mandatorily summoned on two subsequent occasions for witness-identification purposes. The only other time Barbie was seen in the courtroom was to again hear the charges against him and be sentenced.

There was no doubt of Barbie's guilt. A mountain of evidence against him was presented by the prosecutor. Both French Jews and Resistance workers had testified against Barbie: "[From] Barbie's chief victims came a portrait of a particularly brutal fanatic with a taste for sadism. Prosecutor Pierre

Truche said, 'This is not the trial of a German, but of a torturer. It is of a man still loyal to his Nazi ideals.'"[31] He accused Barbie of cruelty far above and beyond the call of duty.

As had been anticipated, Barbie's attorney stressed the extent of French collaboration with the Nazi occupiers. Although it had been feared that this tactic would cause a schism among the French people, the country followed the trial calmly. It was viewed more as a lesson in history rather than a reason for neighbors to turn on one another.

To further dilute Vergés's strategy, the victims' forty lawyers had arranged for silent vigils to be held the day before the trial. One vigil was conducted at a farmhouse near the village of Izieu, where the forty-one Jewish children and those who cared for them were rounded up to be sent to a death camp. The second vigil was conducted at the nineteenth-century dungeonlike prison where Barbie had tortured his victims and ordered executions. At both sites, the lawyers urged unity in fighting Vergés's attempts to divide them. They stressed how essential it was not to deflect attention away from Barbie's wrongdoings.

However, in addition, Vergés also launched a traditional defense of his client, citing inconsistencies in the evidence and testimony presented by the prosecution. Vergés said, "I am not saying this to mock the witnesses, but after forty years, memories become confused."[32] He also insisted that Barbie's expulsion from Bolivia was illegal, and as such, constituted still another "dishonor for France."[33]

Once Vergés completed his closing arguments, the court ordered that Barbie be brought back into the courtroom to hear the three hundred and forty-

A handcuffed Klaus Barbie leaves the French courtroom
where he was tried for war crimes. As there were
death threats against both Barbie and his attorney,
Barbie was protected by armed guards.

one charges against him. Nine jurors and three judges had deliberated for six hours before finding Barbie guilty on all three hundred and forty-one counts of "crimes against humanity"—a charge adopted by the United Nations in 1945 to deal with Nazi atrocities and incorporated into the French penal code in 1964. Barbie appeared tired and drawn, but nevertheless stood expressionless as Presiding Judge André Cerdini read the guilty verdict.

The verdict brought forth a joyous outburst from those present. As the verdict was read, a spontaneous burst of applause and cheers broke out from the spectators jammed together at the back of the courtroom. From outside in the street came more sounds of joy and the sounds of cars honking.

When Barbie's lawyer appeared on the steps of the courthouse, an angry mob began forming. From the crowd came shouts of "SS!" and "Assassin!"[34] Police quickly moved to protect the lawyer.

Klaus Barbie received the maximum penalty for his crimes—he was sentenced to life in prison. As Rabbi Marvin Hier of the Simon Wiesenthal Center in Los Angeles summarized the trial's outcome, "If you choose to be a Gestapo torturer, you eventually pay a price."[35]

5

KURT WALDHEIM

Kurt Waldheim is a tall, slim, stately-looking man who held the prestigious position of secretary-general of the United Nations for two terms, from 1972 to 1982. While at the UN, Waldheim had a reputation in diplomatic circles as an aloof but somewhat effective bureaucrat, and he had managed to achieve good relations with both the United States and the Soviet Union. At the close of his second term as UN secretary-general, Waldheim returned to his native country of Austria, where he launched a campaign to seek the office of president.

Things seemed to be going along well enough for the then sixty-seven-year-old diplomat when a controversy regarding an earlier period in his life publicly exploded, disrupting his campaign and irreconcilably altering the image Kurt Waldheim had long striven to achieve. The international media sizzled with the insinuation that Kurt Waldheim may have distorted information about his background to hide an ugly Nazi past. Was the man who had held an esteemed UN position, and who hoped to be Austria's next president, actually a war criminal?

(129)

Waldheim, who fervently denied any affiliation with the Nazis, claimed that he spent most of the war years as a student. Indeed, throughout the years, his memoirs, resumes, and various interviews all indicated that Kurt Waldheim's military career had ended in 1941, when, after suffering an injury, he returned to Vienna to study law.

However, disturbing facts to the contrary have since come to light. As reported in *Newsweek*,

> The World Jewish Congress (WJC) began uncovering documents showing that Waldheim returned to active service as early as March 1942.
> One such document, dated July 31, 1942, lists him as an interpreter with the intelligence division of the German 12th Army Staff. Waldheim has since admitted that he did serve in the Balkans after 1941—but only as a translator. He also conceded his previous membership in several Hitler youth groups—the Nazi Student Union, the SA (storm troopers) and the N.S. Ruterkorps. But he insists that he viewed them as social clubs and joined only to shield his family.[1]

At one point, Waldheim described the role of these Nazi youth organizations as that of "holding social gatherings, coffee parties, and things like that."[2]

During his tenure at the UN, Waldheim had clung to his story of having spent most of the war studying law after being wounded on the Russian front in 1941. The fact that he had been assigned to the Balkans while he pursued his studies in his spare time was kept even from his closest friends and associates. As Robert Rhodes James, now a member of the British Parliament and formerly a UN speechwriter for Waldheim, described the cover-up: "Waldheim used to sit around in the evenings and

(130)

In 1979 United Nations Secretary-General Kurt Waldheim accepts a kiss from a thirteen-year-old girl. At the time, Waldheim was an internationally respected man— his Nazi background was still a secret.

reminisce about his days at law school in 1943 and 1944. It was lies, all lies. And now I feel betrayed, as does nearly everyone who worked for him then."[3]

The German presence in Yugoslavia during the years in which Waldheim served there was malevolently brutal. The civilian population's Resistance movement had proven itself both courageous and strong, and in return, the Nazis were determined to break people's hope and spirit. It was at this time that the Nazi authorities arranged for reprisal ratios among the local population. They determined that for every German killed, fifty Serbs were to be executed. If a German was wounded, fifty Serbs would be wounded accordingly.

The instructions coming from the commander-in-chief of the 12th Army unit to which Waldheim had been assigned were precise:

> The most minor case of rebellion, resistance, or concealment of arms must be treated immediately by the strongest deterrent methods. The troops must be trained to retaliate with maximum force in these circumstances. The more implacable and explicit the measures adopted henceforth, the less will be the need for them in the future. No sentimentality! It is better to liquidate 50 suspects than to have one soldier killed.[4]

Kurt Waldheim's primary duty within his military unit was supposedly to act as an interpreter between the German and Italian commands. He was fluent in Italian, French, German, and English and had begun to learn Serbo-Croatian. Under the circumstances, it isn't possible that he could have served in the area and been totally unaware of the occupation's violence and brutality, as he later claimed to be.

The tall, thin man in this picture (second from left) is Waldheim. He is shown here in Nazi uniform at an airfield. Despite overwhelming evidence against him, Waldheim continued to deny his participation in Nazi atrocities.

According to an article in *Newsweek,*

There is evidence that [Waldheim] and his intelligence unit produced reports and transmitted orders that were sometimes followed by atrocities. And there is a reason to believe that Waldheim knew about the massacres of civilians in Greece and Yugoslavia, the deportation of Greek Jews and interrogation and murder of Allied POWS. . . . A duty roster dated December 1, 1943, says Waldheim's responsibilities included compiling daily intelligence reports, keeping track of prisoner interrogations and monitoring "special tasks," a common euphemism for torture and execution.[5]

Yet in a television interview on the "CBS Morning News" on March 15, 1986, Waldheim publicly insisted, "It is true that I served in the Balkans, but I never participated in any cruelties."[6]

While acting as an interpreter, Waldheim's immediate supervisor was General Alexander Löhr, a German commander who was later hanged for war crimes. Löhr had overseen the deportation of forty-two thousand Jews from Salonika, Greece, to Nazi death camps. As news sources described Waldheim's role in the process:

While Waldheim was there, thousands of Jews wearing Stars of David passed in and out of Salonika. The World Jewish Congress has uncovered a document informing his intelligence unit that 2,000 Jews had been rounded up. Still, Waldheim says he knew nothing about the deportations. . . . He said he missed one massacre in October 1944 because he had been evacuated 200 miles away before it happened. Survivors say that the massacre took place earlier than Waldheim says. The World Jewish Congress has also found a document carrying Waldheim's signature that describes partisan guerrilla activities.[7]

In a further attack on Waldheim's innocence and credibility, new accusations have been hurled against him from a former member of the Jewish community in Greece. Moshe Myouni is a Greek-born Jew presently residing in Israel. According to Myouni, in the Greek town of Ióannina, Kurt Waldheim actually assisted in rounding up Jews to be transported to German concentration camps for gassing.

Now the owner of a small pastry shop in Tel Aviv, Mr. Myouni claims that an officer he recognizes as Waldheim sent the Jewish prisoners to a transit camp at Lárisa, where he ordered them to surrender their valuables. "He said we wouldn't need them where we were going. The officer also used a stick to strike many of the people, including [my] twenty-three-year-old brother Baruch, who later died at Auschwitz. I knew then I would never forget what this man looked like."[8] Moshe Myouni was more fortunate than many. He escaped shortly before the other prisoners were removed and therefore was able to avoid being killed.

Mr. Myouni recognized Kurt Waldheim from a photograph shown on Israeli television following the public revelation of Waldheim's Nazi affiliations. He said that a distant relative of his recognized Waldheim as well. Moshe Myouni has told his story to Israeli newspapers, a West German magazine, and Greek television. He says he is "one million percent sure" that he has correctly identified the man in question as Kurt Waldheim.

More recently, still other Nazi documents have been located that substantiate charges that Kurt Waldheim's role in World War II was far more than that of a translator. "A personal chart lists Waldheim as the sole chief of 03 intelligence unit and numbers among its duties 'sauberung' (cleansing operations) and 'vernehmung' (interrogations). There is documentation that Waldheim was decorated for his role in the Kozara massacres against Yugoslav partisans."[9]

The award in question, known as the medal of the Order of Zvonimir, was given to Waldheim as a reward for heroic courage in the battle against the rebels during the spring and summer of 1942. This action is better known as the Kozara massacres against the Yugoslav partisans.

On countless occasions, Waldheim has tried to summarily dismiss this dubious distinction, saying that he had done nothing to merit the medal. As cited in the text of *Waldheim*:

> In the apologia he made public on April 12, 1986, the recipient [Waldheim] claimed that this medal was handed out to anyone and everyone, and that it had been awarded to him for exploits prior to his posting to Kozara, despite the fact that the official citation states exactly the opposite. . . . The Order of Zvonimir was not bestowed lightly. It should be added that the decoration he won bore oak leaves, a special mark for acts of bravery under enemy fire.[10]

Adding support to the charges against Waldheim, the investigative research done by University of North Carolina historian Robert Herzstein for the World Jewish Congress revealed documents that conclusively demonstrated "how Waldheim headed an intelligence unit responsible for 'special tasks' on the Balkan Peninsula. In Nazi terms, . . . that meant secret operations, including torture, kidnappings, executions, and burning villages."[11]

To further blacken the gathering cloud of evidence against Waldheim, it was later revealed that the Yugoslavia War Crimes Commission had long ago turned up their own damaging evidence against Waldheim. For example, when questioned as to what Waldheim's duties entailed, Johann Mayer, a fellow officer who served with Waldheim in the Balkans, emphasized "that Waldheim's task was to offer suggestions for reprisals, the fate of the prisoners of war, and imprisoned civilians." Mayer said, "Some of the people executed at Sarajevo in November 1944 received this treatment as the result of an order given by Waldheim in reprisal for the desertion from the German army of several other men." [12]

In view of the substantial documentation, Kurt Waldheim was declared a war criminal by the Yugoslavia War Crimes Commission. In December 1947, they had asked the Allied Commission for his extradition to their country to stand trial.

As stated in *Waldheim*, "On December 12, 1947, the Waldheim file was completed by the commissioner and numbered F-25 572. The cover is inscribed—'Murders and massacres, execution of hostages, destruction of goods by fire.'" [13]

The Allied Commission, for its part, returned the following indictments on February 19, 1948: "Putting hostages to death, murder . . . the mere scope of Kurt Waldheim's job at headquarters was sufficient to prove that reprisals were conducted on his recommendation. Other documents which support this contention exist in Yugoslavia, in private archives." [14]

There is also evidence that the UN was involved in Waldheim's cover-up. According to *Time*:

A U.S. military archivist in Washington stumbled upon a list of the names of all those for whom the UN possesses war crime dossiers. As it turned out, Waldheim's name was on the list. Israel and American Jewish organizations accused the UN of a cover-up and began a campaign to open the archives to public inspection. In October of 1987, the 17 countries of the now disbanded War Crimes Commission agreed.[15]

Despite the massive evidence that had begun to snowball against him, Waldheim continued to claim that he was innocent and had a clear conscience. A rich variety of excuses and disclaimers were always on the tip of his tongue. As *Newsweek* describes his many cover-ups: "When the Nazi atrocities took place, Kurt Waldheim was 100 miles away—or at law school, or recovering from a foot injury. Or he was merely a translator, a desk jockey who knew nothing, heard nothing, saw nothing."[16] That was what Kurt Waldheim wanted the world to believe.

When the U.S. Justice Department initiated a thorough examination of the evidence against him, Waldheim hired a Washington, D.C.–based law firm to represent his interests during the investigation. In an attempt to clear their client, the attorneys at Santarelli, Smith, Kraut, and Carroccio amassed a considerable number of documents to prove Waldheim's innocence.

However, their best efforts were no match for the barrage of incriminating evidence revealed through the Justice Department's yearlong investigation of Waldheim's background. As a spokesperson from the U.S. Department of Justice had announced: "The evidence collected establishes a prima facie case that Kurt Waldheim assisted or otherwise participated in the persecution of peoples because of race, religion, national origin, or political opinion."[17]

The Office of Special Investigations under the Justice Department had compiled a two-hundred-page report substantiating earlier charges against Waldheim. It also brought new evidence to light regarding his wartime activities. Among the most damaging of the current findings was Waldheim's active role in the transfer of four hundred and twenty-eight civilian prisoners to be used as slave labor in the Nazi SS camps.

The investigation also confirmed that Kurt Waldheim played a vital role in the mass deportation to Germany's death camps of Jews and other civilians in Yugoslavia and Greece. He had also been instrumental in the distribution of virulently anti-Semitic propaganda in the Balkans. In addition, the investigation found that Waldheim had turned over Allied prisoners to the Nazi secret service known as the SD. According to a Justice Department official: "The evidence against him was strong enough that had Waldheim been a naturalized U.S. citizen, the government would have moved to deport him—a maneuver requiring proof of guilt beyond a reasonable doubt."[18]

Due to the undeniable conclusion of Waldheim's guilt in this matter, he was placed on a "watch list." This means that the former secretary-general of the United Nations has joined the ranks of the some four hundred thousand criminals, communists, and carriers of contagious disease who are barred from entering the United States.

Despite the ugly reverberations from abroad regarding his past, Waldheim continued his campaign for the presidency of Austria. Apparently, public knowledge of his background did not hinder Waldheim's popularity among the Austrians. After the World War II charges emerged, Waldheim jumped to an eleven-point lead over his opponent in the polls.

Unfortunately, Kurt Waldheim's bid for the presidency coupled with the concerns about his Nazi past served to stir deep feelings of anti-Semitism that apparently were still present in Austria. As described in *Newsweek*:

> Many Austrians—from ordinary workers to influential editors and politicians—have accused the Jews of trying to smear Waldheim and Jewish leaders have received a stream of hate mail, some of it threatening violence if he is defeated. The letters are mostly unsigned and vicious. "What certain Jewish circles are trying to do to Waldheim," says one, "causes me to comment that it is a shame that these criminals weren't gassed by Hitler." . . . Leon Zelman, executive director of the Jewish Welcome Service in Vienna, and other Jewish leaders received a daily stack of angry letters. "Do you want a new Kristallnacht in Vienna?" threatened one, referring to the infamous night in November 1938 when Nazi Brownshirts rampaged through Jewish areas in Germany and Austria.
>
> Another echoed Hitler's xenophobic propaganda: "The Jews were and once again are alien bodies in our people." Still another written by a man who identified himself as a former World War II Army major warned that "if Dr. Waldheim loses the election on May 4th, we will blow up various Jewish facilities and businesses."[19]

As it turned out, Kurt Waldheim won the election. However, his personal future as well as the prestige he can bring to his country internationally has been seriously diminished by the controversy. The World Jewish Congress has promised not to let the issue die.

Although President Waldheim works out of a splendid suite of offices, he finds few visitors eager to meet with him. *Time* reported that when the Swedish foreign minister was asked whether Waldheim would be welcome at the royal court in Stockholm, the gentleman diplomatically replied: "The problem does not arise. His Majesty's program is booked solid for years, and your question is therefore purely academic."[20]

When Pope John Paul granted Waldheim an audience at the Vatican in the summer of 1987, protests were heard from the international Jewish community. Much to his regret, at this point, Kurt Waldheim has largely become an unwelcome visitor abroad as well as an embarrassment to many Austrians. As the controversy over Waldheim's Nazi past has continued to dominate international headlines, some Austrians have called for their president's resignation. However, Waldheim has insisted that he'll complete his term, as he reminded his critics, "I am a President for the Austrians and not for abroad."[21]

A poll taken by a popular Austrian magazine, *Wiener*, revealed that fifty percent of the Austrians surveyed wanted Waldheim to resign.[22] Some Austrians have expressed concern over how having a president with Nazi affiliations may affect Austria's economy. They wish Austria to remain as an attractive tourist resort, a profitable exporter of goods, and an international meeting place. For Austria to do so, they doubt if it can long afford to be indifferent to the sentiments of other nations.

In the interim, Kurt Waldheim's presidency has done little to elevate his nation's status or enhance Austria's image as a civilized and humane community. At times, Waldheim seems oblivious to the insults and insinuations that spring to life as researchers continue to explore his past. It is obvious that he's pleased to be Austria's president despite the internal divisiveness and external loss of status that may result from his tenure in office. As was once said of Waldheim, "He is so thick-skinned that he does not need a backbone to stand erect."[23]

EPILOGUE

According to a survey conducted by the Roper Organization, four out of every five Americans would like to stop being reminded of the Nazi Holocaust. The majority of the Americans surveyed also felt that the Justice Department should not continue its pursuit of Nazi war criminals.[1] One researcher, analyzing the poll results, commented that "there would appear to be a widespread desire to invoke a kind of statute of limitations on being reminded of the Holocaust."[2]

Some people feel the Holocaust occurred too long ago to be of concern to them. They are certain that it could never happen today and certainly not in America. Yet, in 1984–85, members of an Idaho-based group known as The Order committed a string of armored-car robberies to finance an independent Aryan homeland in the Northwest. According to Barry Kowalski, deputy chief of the Justice Department's criminal section: "The plan was to train an army, assassinate primarily Jewish leaders and send a shock message out to the country."[3] Two members of The Order have already been convicted for the murder of Alan Berg, a Jewish radio talk-show host from Denver, Colorado.

Unless the reality and horror of the Holocaust are remembered, and Nazi war criminals are brought to justice, an era of atrocities could repeat itself. As Nazi hunter Beate Klarsfeld stressed: "The trials provide a special education—an awareness of the past—that is vital for young people. It is only in the last decade that the public has learned the uniqueness of [Nazi Germany's] evil plan to annihilate an entire minority."[4]

Simon Wiesenthal has stated that the only punishment he favors for war criminals is that handed out by the courts.[5] To that end, the U.S. Department of Justice has pledged to continue to search for Nazis who have thus far evaded justice. As Neal Sher, the department's head Nazi hunter, reminds us: "Don't ever forget that Charles Manson is considered a mass murderer because he killed six people. That was ten minutes' work in the Holocaust."[6]

SOURCE NOTES

Introduction
1. *America*, 14 June 1986, 492.
2. Luc Rosenzweig and Bernard Cohen, *Waldheim* (New York: Adama Books, 1987).
3. *U.S. News & World Report*, 18 May 1987, 36.
4. *Maclean's*, 25 May 1987, 40.

Chapter 1
1. Benjamin B. Ferencz, *Less Than Slaves* (Cambridge, Mass.: Harvard University Press, 1979), 24.
2. Michael Bar-Zohar, *The Avengers* (London: A. Baker, 1968), 234.
3. Bernd Naumann, *Auschwitz* (London: Pall Mall Press, 1966), 272.
4. Arrest warrant and indictment issued in Frankfort am Main on January 19, 1981, by the Landgericht 22 Strafkammer (State Court Number 22), file number (22)50/LJs340/68.
5. Ibid.
6. Ibid.
7. Gerald L. Posner and John Ware, *Mengele: The Complete Story* (New York: McGraw-Hill, 1986), 45.
8. Ibid., 61.

9. Ibid., 71.
10. Ibid., 164.
11. Ibid., 165.
12. Ibid., 180.
13. Ibid., 191.
14. Naumann, 93.
15. Simon Wiesenthal, *The Murderers Among Us* (London: Heinemann, 1967), 158–159.
16. Benno Weiser Varon, "Living With Mengele," *Midstream*, December 1983, 24.
17. Posner and Ware, 218.
18. Ibid., 221.
19. Ibid.
20. Ibid.
21. Ibid., 222.
22. Posner and Ware, 242.
23. Ibid.
24. Ibid., 258.
25. Ibid., 263.
26. Ibid., 285.
27. *Time*, 26 September 1977, 36–38.
28. Posner and Ware, 297.
29. Ibid., 313.
30. Ibid., 317.

Chapter 2
1. Moshe Pearlman, *The Capture and Trial of Adolf Eichmann* (New York: Simon & Schuster, 1963), 56.
2. Ibid.
3. Ibid., 60.
4. Ibid., 146.
5. Ibid., 149.
6. Ibid.
7. Ibid., 150.
8. Ibid., 168.
9. Ibid., 179.
10. Ibid., 181.
11. Ibid.
12. Ibid., 182.
13. Ibid., 619.

14. Ibid.
15. Ibid., 628.
16. Ibid.
17. Ibid., 629.

Chapter 3
  1. George Szamuelyin, "Did the U.S. Recruit Nazi War Criminals?" *Commentary*, June 1988, 51.
  2. Ibid., 52.
  3. Tom Bowker, *The Paperclip Conspiracy: The Hunt for Nazi Scientists* (Boston: Little, Brown, 1987), 112.
  4. Ibid., 113.
  5. Ibid.
  6. Szamuelyin, 51.
  7. Ibid., 52.
  8. Ibid., 58.
  9. Bowker, 6.
10. William Bole, "Who Helped Nazis Escape to America?" *Present Tense*, July–August 1986, 7.
11. Ibid.
12. Ibid.
13. *The Nation*, 7 June 1986, 792.
14. Ibid.
15. Bole, 7.
16. *Time*, 24 February 1986, 59.
17. Bole, 7.
18. Ibid.
19. *National Catholic Reporter*, 16 May 1986, 24.
20. Ibid.
21. Bole, 8.
22. Ibid.
23. Ibid., 10.
24. *Time*, 20 April 1987, 6.
25. *Newsweek*, 2 March 1987, 36.
26. Ibid.
27. Ibid.
28. *Maclean's*, 25 March 1987, 34.
29. Ibid.
30. Ibid.
31. Bole, 47.

32. Ibid.
33. *U.S. News & World Report*, 2 May 1988, 10.
34. *Newsweek*, 4 May 1987, 34.
35. *The Star Ledger*, 3 May 1990, 4.
36. *Life*, May 1987, 54.
37. Ibid., 55.
38. Ibid.
39. Ibid.
40. Ibid.

Chapter 4
1. Tom Bowker, *Klaus Barbie, the Butcher of Lyons* (New York: Pantheon Books, 1984), 21.
2. Ibid.
3. *Newsweek*, 11 May 1987, 41.
4. Ibid.
5. *U.S. News & World Report*, 18 May 1987, 35.
6. Bowker, 77.
7. Ibid., 132.
8. Ibid.
9. Ibid., 140.
10. Ibid., 164.
11. Ibid., 176.
12. *U.S. News & World Report*, 18 May 1987, 36.
13. Bowker, 13.
14. Ibid., 14.
15. *Time*, 18 May 1987, 49.
16. *U.S. News & World Report*, 18 May 1987, 35.
17. Ibid.
18. *U.S. News & World Report*, 13 July 1987, 16.
19. *U.S. News & World Report*, 13 April 1987, 74.
20. *U.S. News & World Report*, 18 May 1987, 36.
21. *Time*, 18 May 1987, 49.
22. *U.S. News & World Report*, 18 May 1987, 36.
23. *Newsweek*, 11 May 1987, 41.
24. *U.S. News & World Report*, 18 May 1987, 36.
25. *Newsweek*, 20 April 1987, 34.
26. *Newsweek*, 11 May 1987, 41.

27. Ibid.
28. *Time*, 13 July 1987, 40.
29. *Maclean's*, 25 May 1987, 35.
30. Ibid.
31. *Time*, 13 July 1987, 40.
32. Ibid.
33. Ibid.
34. Ibid.
35. *U.S. News & World Report*, 13 July 1987, 16.

Chapter 5
1. *Newsweek*, 5 May 1986, 37.
2. Ibid.
3. *Newsweek*, 9 June 1986, 31.
4. Luc Rosenzweig and Bernard Cohen, *Waldheim* (New York: Adama Books, 1987), 59–60.
5. *Newsweek*, 9 June 1986, 31.
6. Ibid.
7. *Newsweek*, 5 May 1986, 36.
8. *Newsweek*, 19 May 1986, 46.
9. *Newsweek*, 5 May 1986, 37.
10. Rosenzweig and Cohen, 62.
11. *U.S. News & World Report*, 7 April 1986, 10.
12. Rosenzweig and Cohen, 87.
13. Ibid., p. 88.
14. Ibid.
15. *Time*, 7 December 1987, 36.
16. *Newsweek*, 11 May 1987, 40.
17. Ibid.
18. Ibid.
19. *Newsweek*, 5 May 1986, 37.
20. *Time*, 18 January 1988, 34.
21. Ibid.
22. Ibid.
23. *National Review*, 4 July 1986, 17.

Epilogue
1. *The Christian Century*, 1 January 1986, 10.
2. Ibid.

3. *Newsweek*, 19 September 1988, 29.
4. *U.S. News & World Report*, 18 May 1987, 36.
5. *Maclean's*, 25 May 1987, 40.
6. *U.S. News & World Report*, 13 July 1987, 16.

FOR FURTHER READING

Books

Finkelstein, Norman. *Remember Not to Forget: A Memory of the Holocaust*. New York: Franklin Watts, 1985.

Lifton, Robert J. *The Nazi Doctors: Medical Killing and the Psychology of Genocide*. New York: Basic Books, 1986.

Posner, Gerald, and John Ware. *Mengele: The Complete Story*. New York: McGraw-Hill, 1986.

Rossel, Seymour. *The Holocaust*. New York: Franklin Watts, 1981.

Ryan, Allan A. *Quiet Neighbors: Prosecuting Nazi War Criminals in America*. New York: Harcourt, 1984.

Sender, Ruth. *The Cage*. New York: Macmillan, 1986.

Shavin, Amir. *Ivan the Terrible: The Demjanjuk Trial*. New York: Adama Books, 1987.

Werbell, Frederick, and Thurston Clarke. *Lost Hero: The Mystery of Raoul Wallenberg*. New York: McGraw Hill, 1981.

Wiesenthal, Simon. *Every Day Remembrance Day: A Chronicle of Jewish Martyrdom*. New York: H. Holt, 1987.

Articles

Barnes, Edward. "Accused: 28 Years a U.S. Citizen, Bohdan Kozly Is Suspected of Killing Jews in World War II." *Life*, May 1987.

Coleman, Fred. "The Barbie Trial: J'accuse: A Living Witness to the Gestapo Chief's Crimes." *Newsweek*, May 11, 1987.

"A French Cellar Dweller." (Nazi collaborator, fugitive from justice) *U.S. News & World Report*, June 5, 1989.

Goldin, Milton. "Profits of Doom: How the Nazis Killed Six Million Jews and Made Money, Too." *Present Tense*, March–April 1988.

Greenwald, John. "In Search of the Smoking Gun: A Historian Claims New Evidence Links Waldheim to Atrocities." *Time*, February 8, 1988.

Greenwald, John. "Trapped in the Eye of the Storm: An Ever More Isolated Waldheim Awaits the Historians' Verdict." *Time*, January 18, 1988.

Harriman, Ed. "A Cupboard Full of Nazis." *New Statesman & Society*, August 5, 1988.

Harrison, Barbara. "Selected Memories: What Time Refuses to Forget: the Waldheim Affair." *Commonweal*, June 6, 1986.

"It's Not Easy to Embarrass the United Nations." (Notebook—opening of Nazi war criminal file.) *The New Republic*, October 26, 1987.

Morgan, Ted. "The Barbie File." *New York Times Magazine*, May 10, 1987.

"Nazi Assets." (U.S. Army Intelligence recruited Nazis after World War II.) Editorial, *The Nation*, July 2, 1988.

"Nazi Trail: Opening the U.N. Files." (UN dossiers on war criminals.) *Time*, December 7, 1987.

Nicholas, Mark. "Unveiling a Hidden Past." *Maclean's*, March 17, 1986.

Nordland, Rod. "Waldheim: New Links to Nazi Past." *Newsweek*, April 7, 1986.

"Put Nazis on Trial: Never Forget What They Did." Editorial, *The Economist*, December 16, 1989.

Smith, Chris. "Remembering Kristallnacht." (Anniversary of Nazi riot against Jews.) *New York Times*, November 7, 1988.

Szamuelyin, George. "Did the U.S. Recruit Nazi War Criminals?" *Commentary*, June 1988.

"An Unrepentent Nazi." (Alois Brunner extradition sought.) *Maclean's*, November 11, 1985.

Walmsley, Ann, and Sue Masterman. "Stalking the Nazis." (Simon Wiesenthal.) *Maclean's*, December 9, 1985.

INDEX

ABOUT THE AUTHOR

Elaine Landau received a B.A. degree in English and Journalism from New York University, and a master's degree in Library and Information Science from Pratt Institute.

Ms. Landau has worked as a newspaper reporter, an editor, and a youth services librarian. She has written many books and articles on contemporary issues for young people. Ms. Landau lives in New Jersey.